Kevin Costner
Prince of Hollywood

Kelvin Caddies

Plexus, London

For my mother Margaret, and Anita,
for their love, understanding and support –
not only for 'the book'.

Text copyright © 1992 by Kelvin Caddies
Published by Plexus Publishing Limited
26 Dafforne Road
London SW17 8TZ
First printing 1992

Caddies, Kelvin
    Kevin Costner: Prince of Hollywood
    I. Title
    791.43028092

    ISBN 0 85965 109 6

Printed and bound in Hong Kong
Cover and book design by Simon Bell

1 2 3 4 5 6 7 8 9

Contents

Introduction   4

1   Chasing Dreams   7

2   No Way Out   25

3   Untouchable   45

4   Dances With Wolves   73

5   Prince of Hollywood   87

6   American Flyer   99

7   Moving On   111

Filmography   126

Acknowledgements   128

Introduction

KEVIN COSTNER only came into the movies in 1979, yet few stars can match the impact he had already made in little more than a decade. Who can forget Kevin Costner as the crusading District Attorney in *JFK,* who defied the powers of government and tried to prove there was a conspiracy to kill President John F. Kennedy? He was equally arresting in such disparate roles as the dashing young nobleman fighting to free his country from poverty and persecution in *Robin Hood: Prince of Thieves*; the soldier in search of his destiny living among the Sioux Nation in *Dances With Wolves*; the farmer with a vision of building a baseball park in *Field Of Dreams*; the crime-busting cop out to clean up prohibition Chicago in *The Untouchables*...

Like the characters he portrays on screen, Kevin Costner has been described as straight and honest; the guy-next-door whom men look up to - and women fall for. He has classic good looks, a soft-spoken man of action rather than words in his films. He radiates the charisma of Gary Cooper, the charm of Robert Redford, the vulnerability of Henry Fonda and the wholesomeness of James Stewart; a clean-cut throwback hero in the great tradition of Hollywood, who fulfils many of the same ideals now that those stars did for their generation. To many he is the epitome of the great American dream.

But behind Kevin Costner's 'Aw shucks' air lies a shrewd businessman, a perfectionist who admits to having dark sides to his personality. His easy going manner conceals a driven man with very definite ideas about what he wants; a hard-edged, sometimes ruthless character disguised behind the boyish grin. How else could a bit-part actor who was cut out of many of his early movies climb so swiftly to become the world's Number One superstar and one of the most powerful people in the film industry; a novice who graduated from a series of sexploitation romps to become the producer, director and star of a film that carried away seven Academy Awards and made over half a billion dollars? And all by the age of 36!

What makes the story of Kevin Costner more remarkable is that from his humble beginnings, right through childhood and college until early adulthood, he was a loner, a self-admitted 'outsider' and 'plodder' who was awkward, shy and lived in awe of his disciplinarian father. Even the thought of becoming an actor didn't occur to him until he was in his twenties.

Kevin Costner has taken some knocks along with the adulation, and his personal life has come under the media microscope. Perhaps the openness of the ordinary father and husband living in a middle-class suburb of Hollywood in the early 1980s could never survive the sudden success of later years. Costner has drawn in his horns, and a new guardedness could be detected in his public persona. But the facts of his life and career reveal much about the motivation and dedication of this exceptional star.

Chapter One

Chasing Dreams

He was a small, scrawny boy, with a lopsided smile and the bright, cunning eyes of his native American forefathers. He was wearing tattered dungarees, muddy knees protruding through frayed gashes at the legs, a home-made bow and arrow slung over his left shoulder, a rabbit and two squirrels dancing lifelessly from a rope hooked to his belt. Heart thumping, the ten-year-old hunter scurried through the woods surrounding the outskirts of Los Angeles, anxious to get home before his father returned from work, eager to show him the kills.

Revelling in the escapist fantasy of a natural born loner who would one day grow up and live out his Wild West dreams on screen, Kevin Costner was remarkably resourceful as a child. In kindergarten, when he wasn't scrapping with classmates and being sent to the principal's office, he was pitching stones at oil rigs as they passed the school with a catapult he had made from a forked twig and a piece of innertube from a car tyre. For his fifth birthday, he was given his first gun – a big Winchester BB – and taught how to shoot by his father in their backyard, using tin cans and bottles for target practice. 'From the time my brother and I were seven or eight, we had guns, and Dad, he'd set the guns out, and away we'd go, up into the hills together, the three of us,' he recalled. 'I remember private time as a kid, just sitting down with my gun. It's a wonder I'm still alive. I used to get into tunnels, in irrigation ditches. I had no idea where I was gonna end up. I was real adventurous that way. My mother wouldn't see me until I came back and it was dark. The only require-ment was, "Don't go in your school clothes."'

But it was the bow and arrow which

became the young Costner's favoured weapon, because the deadly silence of an arrow would not alert and scare off any other prey. He made them himself from well-seasoned wood cut from the birch and willow trees which grew plentifully in the region. Using a knife to whittle the bow into shape, he would rub it all over with oil or animal fat to make it more durable, then stretch a bowstring across it made from rawhide. Duck feathers were used for the arrow flights, pieces of tin hammered into surgical-sharp arrowheads.

At the most exciting moment of the hunt, as he crouched unseen behind some saplings, aiming his arrow at an unsuspecting squirrel or rabbit that had taken the bait, the young boy felt deliriously happy. The exciting smell of the undergrowth, the pine-needle covered ground, birds squawking overheard, filled him with a longing always to be close to the wilds of nature, and a deep love for the outdoors would stir within him. For the rest of his life, the sights and sounds of the forest brought back an instant, vivid image of his childhood.

Kevin Costner was born on 18 January 1955, in Lynwood, a lower-income Los Angeles suburb, and raised in neighbouring Compton. He was the youngest of two sons, his older brother Dan having been born in 1950. Another brother, Mark, died at birth in 1953. His parents moved there from Oklahoma after his half-Cherokee grandparents on his father's side (Costner is also of Irish and German descent) lost the family farm during the great Mid-West dust bowl disaster. Major dust storms ravaged the U.S. prairie states from Kansas to Texas in the 1930s, causing severe soil erosion and drought.

Growing up in grimy Compton was 'like Newark or Harlem' Costner has said, and his family were as poor as any ghetto dwellers. 'My father's side of the family lost everything along with the farm. They were Okies, like the people in *The Grapes Of Wrath*. All they arrived with was a Model A Ford and the few possessions they could carry with them. What that gave us was a real common-sense approach to things. And there's this real need for financial security even now, when I've got more than I ever thought I would.'

After an exhaustive search for work and a brief spell digging ditches, Bill Costner finally found permanent employment as a utilities executive with Southern California Edison. As he serviced their electrical lines, it sometimes became necessary for him to be transferred to other parts of California, such as Santa Paula, Ojai and Ventura, but the constant relocations were a terrible upheaval for his family. Kevin recalls moving schools four times between the ninth and twelfth grades, and he made no real friends; schools were already in session, and Costner was the new boy, shut out from the friendships that had already been formed. He became invisible. 'Those were unstable years,' he said. 'I was always the new kid on the block because we moved so damn much. I was always trying to make new friends each year, and I was never in the clique, which looked pretty appealing from outside. I was like an army child, I didn't want to try and be too funny, I didn't want to try and be too strong, and I didn't want to try and be too good. It was hard, so I gave up trying altogether. I was always on the outside. I didn't feel "there" until the end of the year, and then we'd move again. I lost a lot of confidence in who I was.'

The rabbits and squirrels Costner caught with his bow and arrow often provided food for his family for days; the pelts he would sell in the school playground the next day. The money he made was a further contribution to alleviate his family's dire financial situation. It was his father that gave Costner this strong sense of family duty as a child. 'I desperately wanted to be liked by my dad most of all. And I still do. As a kid, when my dad was coming home from work my brother and I used to wait for him and we used to race to undo the laces of his boots. I wanted so much to please him. My dad was a tremendous influence on me, and I still talk to him nearly every day.'

But this unusually close bond between father and son may well have been formed out of necessity, rather than choice. With the constant moves Bill Costner made few friends apart from work colleagues and acquaintances. When Kevin's brother Dan was drafted into the U.S. marine corps and sent to Vietnam in 1968, their shared loss brought father and younger son even closer. Then aged 13, Kevin tried to compile a book based on letters and tapes Dan sent back from Vietnam. Dan, who was twice awarded gallantry medals, recalled the day Kevin came up to him and said he wanted to write about the white working-class experience in the Vietnam War: 'I was surprised that he was interested.'

According to Bill Costner, however, Kevin's stubborn determination to follow things through once his heart was set on something became evident even earlier than that. 'From day one, Kevin was his own person. Once he decided to take charge of organizing a parade at school. I figured it was too big a job for an 11-year-old and said "Kevin, you can't do that." And Kevin looked up at me with this look in his eyes and said, "Dad, never tell me I'm not able to do something." He went ahead and organized the parade.'

Even so, Kevin was still a constant source of worry for his parents. Always the loner, he would while away the long evenings writing short stories or sit out on the porch day dreaming about the escapades of his favourite film heroes. 'I'd lose myself in the movies,' he said. 'I had a very active fantasy life. I can remember as a ten-year-old watching *How The West Was Won*, and certain moments made me tingle with the magic of it. I didn't want to be an actor then, never even thought about it. But looking back, I think the signs were all there – the singing in the choir, the church musicians, the poetry, the creative writing classes – a constant urge to do that kind of thing.'

In the summer vacations, he would take off on his own and go back-packing, often camping out at nights. 'When I was 18, I split L.A. and built a canoe, which I paddled down the rivers Lewis and Clark navigated while they were making their way to the Pacific. I was just your average hunting, shooting and fishing type kid, I guess,' he has said. It is possible his intention was to alienate his classmates so that they would leave him alone, most certainly because he was acutely self-conscious about his lack of height and feared being the subject of ridicule and torment. Equally it may have been his way of showing he was just as tough as the larger boys.

To say that Costner was small as a teenager was an understatement – he was the smallest boy in his high school class. At 18 he was only 5ft 2in, a misfit who got ignored by girls and didn't have one date during his school days. 'I was a tongue-tied teenager looking up to almost everyone. I was a real late bloomer. Small, gangly with a giant 9½ shoe size. My mom kept assuring me that I would eventually grow. But I never got over being short.' Costner remembers with embarrassment how naive he was as a youth. 'I remember I was in the seventh or eighth grade in high school. This guy was sitting next to me, and he said he balled this girl, and I looked at him, and I said, "Yeah, okay." Then he says, "I really balled her". I was glad I didn't say anything, because two days later I figured out what "balled" meant, and I never forgot that, because I realized how stupid I am about things. I think I've always been a turtle, a plodder.'

Determined to drag him out of his self-imposed shell, it was his welfare-worker mother who had encouraged Kevin to join the school choir and write poetry. Eventually he also became Villa Park High School's top sports star at basketball, baseball and American football. 'I think I like sports because of my father. He never insisted I play with him, which made it even more attractive. He's my idea of how a father should direct his son. Sport, besides the obvious competitive aspect, is about sharing and being fair. He was my teacher and he taught me about loyalty and friendship and doing your best. It's not a Boy Scout creed. Truth and those things are never far out of style.'

In 1973, at the age of 18, Costner enrolled at California State University at Fullerton on a five-year business studies course. Not knowing what he wanted to do with his life,

he figured he may as well try marketing and finance as it seemed to offer a fair number of openings and decent career prospects at the end if he lasted the course. 'All my life, I wanted to meet interesting people, the sort you read about in magazines. My dad told me that my greatest chance of doing that was to find my line of work and do it well. He said whether it was construction, or whether it was being an architect, whatever it was, if I really did it well, then that was my chance for getting on in life. Not just looking at some magazine, and trying to emulate someone else I was reading about. He's a really smart man, my dad.'

Growing up as a child, Costner often dreamed that maybe one day he would be someone special, but it never occurred to him that there could be a future for him in films; that was always something other people did, the lucky ones…and certainly not a poor boy from Compton. 'Movies have always had an impact on me, but I never realistically thought I'd be in them,' he has said. 'I thought those people were somehow born on the screen. I didn't know where they came from.' There were no high school plays, college drama classes or anything similar to fuel his interest. He was 22 when he decided to be an actor. 'By then, especially in America, you are supposed to know what you're doing. There's a notion that people know what they are supposed to do by the

Kevin Costner's adolescence was revealed in pictures in *The People* in 1991. At 18 he was still only 5ft 2in, a loner who suffered an acute inferiority complex about his lack of height.

FROM MY FAMILY ALBUM

Who am I?

A MUCH celebrated Hollywood hunk (who also directs and produces), he used to make his own bows and arrows and shoot rabbits and squirrels in Oklahoma. Married for 13 years he has three kids and speaks the Sioux dialect. He denies having a fling with a Stringfellows PR but admits his income has risen by £5 million in recent months. As a struggling actor he supported his wife as a cook on a deep-sea fishing boat. He may be shy, but he was happy to take MARK THOMAS through his picture album.

HERE I am, 21 years ago as a tongue-tied teenager looking up to almost everyone. I was a real late bloomer. A mere 5ft 2in tall and a giant 9½ shoe size. Yeah, I was shy. Am I the dream of millions of adoring female fans? I didn't go on dates with girls then because they were all taller than me.

THIS was when I enrolled at California State University in 1973 on a five-year business studies course. God, don't I look the little rat, with lapels you could land a light aircraft on. My first theatre role was as Rumpelstiltskin, and I got to where I am today through playing bit parts. All I can remember is that I wanted to please.

AT 18 I was a loner. I built a canoe and set off on my own voyage of discovery down local rivers. Then amazement! I started to grow. At 21 I was 6ft 1in tall, but still very shy. And then I met the student I fell head over heels in love with and later married when I was 23. I was still a virgin. She was only my second date.

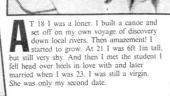

MY father Bill had to keep moving for his job with the telephone company. I was never at any school long enough to make any real friends. I threw myself into sport and became a star player at basketball and baseball. On the field I used to impersonate actors, TV personalities, our coach and other players. I was moved to Southern California after my family lost their farm in Oklahoma. They arrived in the West with all their possessions packed in the back of a Model A Ford.

The evenings were long so I used my imagination and wrote short stories.

time they get out of college. And I bought into that system. I knew kids who, when they were 12, wanted to be dentists or lawyers. But I never sat down and had a big talk with myself about what I thought I was going to be.'

Costner continued: 'Looking back, I can see that I was always performance-orientated, and I could always see the drama, or the humour, in whatever was going on. But the idea of making acting a living never even occurred to me, because nobody in the family was in that line of business. I didn't have examples to make me think a movie star is what I would become.'

Although Costner tried hard to cultivate an interest in his business studies course, he experienced a growing discontent, a deep-rooted fear that something was missing, and it made him feel hollow. Indeed the thought of his life all mapped out for him, with his college course crowned by graduation, followed by a secure job with a respectable company, appalled him. He had never imagined being tied down before. He thought of the long, dreary years ahead slaving away behind a desk, always answerable to someone else, always at their beck and call...Mr Anonymous. Costner has said: 'I knew I wasn't a suit man, a nine-to-five salesman. So I started listening to my inner voice and said, "You better do it, man". The one voice says, "Grow up", the other says, "Do the most ridiculous thing possible."'

Around that time a notice in the college newspaper caught his attention: the South-coast Actors Co-op were putting on a stage production of *Rumpelstiltskin*, and they wanted people to try out for parts. 'I didn't know my fairy-tales very well but I figured,

"There must be a prince in it. Every fairy-tale has a prince".' Curious, he went along to the audition – but he didn't get the part. 'The casting director looked me straight in the eye and she said, "Well, we're really looking for somebody good-looking." But I knew after I had been in the room with the actors and stage people that this was where I belonged, and I studied acting five nights a week in my spare time after college.'

For the moment, Costner was content to balance his business studies with the acting classes. He still had another three years to finish at college and only time would tell if he had the necessary talent to succeed in showbusiness. There was no point in rushing into things yet. In the meantime, he was eager to learn as much as he could of this interesting new craft.

Although he had a late growth spurt to his present height by the time he was 21, Costner was still painfully shy and has admitted he picked up 'sluts' as a college boy because they were easier to talk to than proper dates, something, he claimed, his mother had told him to do. 'Suddenly I started to grow and girls began to notice me,' Costner said. 'But inside I still felt like a small boy so I was very shy with them and never dated until I got to college when I went wild. I'd never dated much other than recreational dating, because Mother always said never date a girl you wouldn't consider marrying. Saturday night showed up and guys went into a panic if they didn't have a date. I never went through that. I just picked up sluts. I could talk to them. I felt more comfortable about sex that way. You couldn't call them affairs. They were more like collisions.'

These remarks of Costner's have led to some confusion; he has also said that he was a virgin when he married his college sweetheart Cindy, and that she was only his second date. When pressed by Edward Klein in *Vanity Fair* in 1991, Costner admitted that he 'had slept with girls before I married. But not that many.' He added: 'That's why I don't have much sympathy for those high-school movies in which the kid can't get laid. Hell, I couldn't either.'

Costner first met his future wife in March 1975 at a college party. Cindy Silva, four years younger than he, was a biology student who used to spend her summer vacations playing Snow White at Disneyland. She also had a steady boyfriend at the time. 'It was kind of an awkward night for me,' she explained, 'because I was seeing another boy at the time and I went to the party with his sister. Then I saw Kevin. He asked me to dance and then he went away and then we danced again and then he went away again. We danced five times this way. He was wearing penny loafers, his hair was slicked back, he had a sweater over his shoulders, and he looked so sweet. I went home and woke up my mother.'

Costner was immediately attracted to her as well. She looked radiant in a simple linen dress, trim and elegant. 'When Cindy walked in...she was so beautiful, so decent, there was such a glow about her. She had these big, dear eyes. But I didn't think she had even noticed me. I thought Snow White would never look at a guy like me – a little rat from Compton. I wasn't Prince Charming. I had longer hair and wire-rimmed glasses. When I met Cindy it was love at first sight, though even then I was kind of slow getting moving

on it.' Lost for words, dragging his heels, Costner had been distraught to see Cindy leave at the end of the night without first securing a date with her. Returning to his room on the campus, he had cursed himself for letting the opportunity slip by. Unbeknownst to him, Cindy had also felt the same way as he did. Eventually, her Prince Charming plucked up his courage and asked to see her again. 'It took me a month to figure I might have a chance. After that I didn't look at another woman.'

By the end of April, Kevin's persistence had paid off and he and Cindy had become a couple. She was different to any other girl he had ever met before: sophisticated, confident, yet simple and down to earth. Neither of them had much money, so flashy restaurants, the theatre – the kind of places Costner thought he was expected to take a girl on a date – were out of the question. And yet Cindy was happy just to go for walks in the park or spend the day along a river bank, a willing pupil as Kevin tried to teach her how to fish for salmon, just like his father had taught him. She was open and warm and alive, sharing herself, enjoying life, making sure that he enjoyed it too. She brought a new vitality to him, a sense of being, of purpose. And he never wanted it to end.

He could hardly wait to get the approval of his family. 'We were on our way to the movies to see *Funny Girl,* and on the way I took her home to meet my parents. I was just really proud that this girl would go out with me. I wanted to show my parents, "See, I'm not such a fuck up".'

Costner graduated in 1978 with an honours degree in business studies – and married Cindy shortly afterwards. He was 23.

Until then he had managed to suppress his growing urge to take acting further. Two weeks into a marketing job in Orange County that he already hated, and with some promising reviews in Workshop plays to bolster his confidence, Costner was on the verge of making the decision to change the course of his life. That decision was helped along when Kevin and Cindy found they were travelling on the same plane as Richard Burton when returning from their honeymoon in Puerto Vallarta, Mexico.

Glancing across the aisle to make sure that the stewardess had not seen him, full of trepidation about what he was about to do, Costner had stepped through into the first class section, approached the famous actor, and somehow managed to keep a conversation going with Burton for half an hour. Looking back, Costner now believes that their meeting was more than just coincidental: 'I thought Burton was placed on that plane for me to talk to – but he had bought all the seats around him. I finally went up to him and said, "I'd like to ask you for a bit of advice." We got personal very quickly. I wanted to know if he thought it was possible to be essentially a good man and still be in this business. He said that he thought so, and that I should try. He also said, "You've got green eyes, haven't you? I've got green eyes too." The thing I liked about him was he never said it was a hard life, he never said the obvious. After that I had a very clear idea of what I wanted to do. I told Cindy we were going to Hollywood and that if I had to get a job taking out trash, it was going to be movie trash.'

After just 30 days in his first job in marketing, Costner followed through with

his pledge and resigned. As he remembered it, 'My bride took it well, considering. Everybody in our circle thought I was going to be a businessman, and now here I was acting strange and talking about going to Hollywood to break into movies.' According to Cindy, however, who hadn't really taken her impetuous husband seriously, she had been furious when Costner suddenly announced one night that he had given up his job. 'I came home and he was sitting at the table with an old typewriter and a pile of papers. He said, "Well I quit today. I'm going to become an actor and a writer". I just threw all the papers on the floor and screamed at him: "A *writer!* – but you can't even spell!"'

Bill Costner too had deep misgivings about the direction his son was taking. 'My father took it pretty well, but I know he was concerned,' Kevin recalled. 'He really didn't know how to support me. Like a lot of fathers, he wanted to help his children, and when I went into this business, he felt that there was nothing he could offer his son, which was a disappointment to him. And a fear, too, because without his help, he knew I was kind of out there on my own.'

Throughout his formative years Kevin had lived in awe of his father. Conventional and even lecturing at times, Bill Costner was a man of old world attitudes and he found it hard to come to terms with his son's acting aspirations. How Kevin could simply throw

Kevin Costner with his wife Cindy. Although she was happy to stay behind the scenes, there is no doubt that she was a driving force in his life in the early years and helped him achieve his acting ambition.

away the opportunity of achieving a respectable career, and especially after having studied hard for years to get the chance, was beyond him. Bill Costner had always kept a firm grip on his children's lives and never allowed them to be arrogant or big-headed. At one basketball game when Kevin was a teenager, Bill Costner had been horrified to see his son show off in front of his peers. 'I had the exhibitionism knocked out of me,' Kevin recalled. 'During one basketball game, I was knocked into the lap of a pretty girl. She was drinking Coke, and I took a sip. There was a rousing cheer. Later my dad told me, "You're out there to play."'

But Kevin remained resolute about switching careers in mid-stream. 'There I was in marketing. A white rat could have been doing my job. I thought it was time I took some control over my life.' He had always felt he could act, but it was a huge gamble to give up his job like that without having any connections in the business – never mind finding an agent first. 'I guess I took a risk. But I felt it was a bigger risk not to do what I felt was right in my mind and my heart. If acting is in your soul, you can't give it up. Some people are born to it. That's the way I felt. It was a time of my life when I got rock solid with what I wanted to do with my life.' It was as if a large burden had been lifted from his shoulders. He added: 'I never breathed an easier breath. I relaxed then. Then all I had to do was learn. I never felt like turning back, ever.'

Kevin Costner made plans to move to Hollywood straight away, impatient to get going now that he had made his choice. At the same time he kept wondering what his next move would be when he and Cindy reached their destination. 'I've always been outside the movie industry,' he has said. 'When I finally decided to become an actor I didn't even know how one would begin. You live in an area called the Movie Capital of the World but it was foreign to me. It seemed like an impenetrable thing.'

Back in the late 1970s Hollywood was a vibrant, bustling centre of activity, a mecca attracting a continuous flow of migratory, would-be stars like a magnet. Seeking fame and fortune, but disillusioned with the endless bad breaks, those once wide-eyed, hopeful young actors would move on again, their dreams crushed, only to be replaced by more innocent, nameless faces.

Kevin Costner had his dreams too. For hours on end he would walk the city, watching, listening, learning; his mind a safe deposit vault, storing away the information: absorbing everything. He walked along Hollywood Boulevard, peering down studiously at the Walk of Fame, the bronze-and-pink terrazzo stars embedded on the pavement, each with their own legendary name: John Wayne and Elizabeth Taylor, Cary Grant and Clark Gable...almost two thousand he had counted, a galaxy thought to expand by a dozen or so every year. On he went past the locked gates of Universal Film Studios and Columbia and Warner Brothers, shrinking when he saw Barbra Streisand step out of the Regent Beverly-Wilshire Hotel, gawping at the $13,000 price-tag on an Armani suit in Maxfields, the top people's store on Melrose – supermarkets, diners, movie theatres, amusement arcades – everything seemed to be open and available 24 hours a day. It was a heady time for Costner. This was where he was meant to come. He would prove his parents wrong, Cindy, their friends, all the people who had doubted him, the ones who didn't understand.

But first he had to find a job.

Breaking through had been tougher than Costner had imagined. With their savings dwindling away, to help make ends meet, Cindy worked as a member of the ground-staff of Delta Airlines, while he did a variety of odd jobs such as driving a delivery truck, packing crates at an ice-house and working as a chef-deckhand on a deep-sea fishing boat operating out of San Pedro Bay, the seaport of Los Angeles. He would turn his hand to anything to keep them afloat and his dreams alive. Then bad luck struck. Cindy was knocked off her bicycle in a road accident; although she was unhurt, their only form of transport was damaged beyond repair. When they went to the bank to withdraw money to buy a new bike, they were shocked to find that they had only $13 remaining in their account. 'I certainly didn't feel very much like a success at that point in my life,' Costner recalled. 'As a man I was supposed to be the provider. But even then I felt I needed to live like that for a time to become the man I really wanted to be.'

He added: 'Not many women would have understood that. But Cindy convinced me that if we were eating we were okay. When we look back at those days, we realise how far we've come.'

Costner scores at basketball. An accomplished athlete, Costner compensated for his lack of height at high school by excelling at basketball, baseball and American football, eventually becoming his school sports champion.

Costner was also a tour guide on the buses that went along the Pacific Coast Highway from Los Angeles to San Francisco, and the sightseeing tours that took people past the stars' homes in Bel-Air and Beverly Hills. Always clever with his hands, he had also tried carpentry. 'Kevin said two things were going to happen,' recalled the architect for whom Costner once worked in one of his many short-term money-making jobs. 'First, he said he was going to make it big in acting, and, second, he said that he'd have me design a house for them.' They were both promises Costner would eventually keep.

And all the while he continued to go to acting classes in his spare-time after work. For days he would go on like this, often collapsing with exhaustion at the end of the week. Wary of his portfolio being 'lost in the post', Costner did not rely on sending resumés or portrait shots of himself through the mail to casting directors and agents; he almost always appeared in person. 'I'd walk out of their offices with my fingers in my ears so I wouldn't have to hear someone who didn't know as much as I did telling me what to do,' he remembered.

One agent told him brazenly: 'Look, Donald Pleasance will make more money for me this year than you will ever make in this business.' But still he persisted. 'I spent all my time auditioning, and looking for work in the industry – something that would keep me close to acting,' he said. At every audition, there was always a queue, sometimes right outside the door, a crowd of anxious young hopefuls like himself, living on the fringe of stardom, whispering nervously amongst each other in eager anticipation. Often they would go to a nearby bar afterwards, bolstering each other's self-confidence after yet another rejection. 'The doubt of success crept in – I was the kid in the backseat asking "When are we going to get there?" – but I never questioned being on the right road. That's the fun part. If you're obsessed with your destination, you miss 80% of the point of acting: the ride there, the people you meet along the way.'

By the middle of 1979, things had become increasingly worse. Then, after six jobless months, and a period sleeping rough in the back of a truck in a car park, Costner's luck finally changed and he became stage manager at a small independent studio named Raleigh Studios (a decade later he would return and set up his own production company there). 'I had a big debate with myself over whether I should tell my employers that I was an actor,' Costner said. 'Although I called myself an actor, I didn't have an agent and I'd never been interviewed for a professional acting job. In the end I told them – and they still hired me.'

The easy-going atmosphere and adaptable hours at Raleigh gave Costner time to attend drama workshops as well as his acting classes; just as important, it also gave him the opportunity to learn the skills involved behind the scenes of a production studio, such as directing, editing, and camera work. Before long he was assisting the technician lighting the set, helping out the director on a shoot, learning the details of developing film in the red glow of the process lab: 'I spent my time watching other people, it was really a good education for me, and also a technical one.' After a brief foray in front of the camera himself, starring in a short-lived computer commercial made by Raleigh, Costner was approached by his acting teacher, Richard

Brander, whose Studio City workshop he attended, and offered his first movie roles in two low-budget projects. These were being set up by a small production company called Troma Films, now afforded cult status by aficionados of 'schlock' movies.

'Kevin's dedication was far superior to anyone I've ever had in class,' Brander remembered. 'There was a compulsion to learn and an acute self-awareness.' Eager for experience, Costner had jumped at the chance to appear in what would later emerge as nothing but a couple of un-inspiring, sexploitation romps which should have vanished without trace. However, both *Sizzle Beach, USA* and *Shadows Run Black* would re-surface again twelve years later to cash in on

Hungry for success, Costner was happy to pose for photographers at home when he was starting out. When fame finally came his way, the publicity-shy star would try to prevent all intrusions into his private life.

Costner's success at the Oscars with *Dances With Wolves*, while at the same time resulting in a great deal of damaging publicity for the star. 'I felt I really had the chance to become something, but these movies were definitely not the way!' Costner said in 1991.

Directed by Richard Brander, *Sizzle Beach, USA* (originally titled *Malibu Hot Summer*) is a misleading title; although it stars a trio of scantily clad California girls living in a Malibu beach house, it's not a beach movie. The storyline revolves around the girls, who meet each other on their way to LA and decide to stick together. As strangers in a new and possibly unsafe city, they reason it would be in their own interest if they could count on each other until at least they learned their way around.

Sheryl (Leslie Brander, the director's wife) is a big-busted, blonde, fitness fanatic who almost immediately lands a job teaching P.E. at the local high school, with the help of an investment broker she runs into whilst jogging on the beach. Janice (Terry Congie) is a throw back to the sixties, a quirky, hippy flower child who switches into Earth Mother mode with annoying frequency, strumming her guitar and singing wispy folk songs. Encouraged by her flatmates, she heads for a local recording studio with the intention of making a demo tape. Since the studio owner doesn't show much interest in her musical abilities, she takes off with his cousin Steve, a well-built beach hunk the girls later share the house with. Dit (Roselyn Royce) has aspirations to become an actress; driven by an obsession she has for Bette Davis, she takes acting lessons. For recreation, she goes horse riding at a nearby stud farm. Enter the 'stud' on the farm, the wealthy owner with an almost insatiable libido, John Logan (played by Costner). It's not long before he's making hay with Dit (and later Sheryl), and her friends are going equally haywire with each of their 'love interests'.

Branded a 'porno flick' by *The Washington Post*, and disowned by Costner, who later described it as a 'real tits'n'bums affair', *Sizzle Beach, USA* was first shown at the Cannes Film Festival in May 1986, seven years after it was made, and to unanimously scathing attacks from critics. *Variety* wrote: 'Female nudity is plentiful, since every scene is aimed at getting one of the leads to take her clothes off.' As for the actual camera work, it noted: 'Lensing is strictly home-movie level.' However Costner, who was paid around $500 for his role, could take some consolation from *Variety's* overall verdict on the acting abilities of all involved: 'Thespian, apart from Costner, ranges from amateur to atrocious.'

There was more ridicule for Costner, when his follow-up film, the slasher movie *Shadows Run Black* was released (straight onto video, and in 1984). It was a tacky serial killer chiller with a psycho – dubbed 'The Black Angel' by the press – preying on pretty young students...but not before they first remove certain items of underclothing in full view of the camera. Cop on the case, Sergeant Rydell King (William J. Kulzer) is clinically and methodically following up the multiple killings, spurred on by the disappearance of his own teenage daughter, the victim of a 'coincidental' kidnapping. Chief suspect Jimmy Scott (Costner) is an obnoxious thug who knew the victims. However, after he's arrested, the murders are still mounting up. From here on, *Shadows Run Black* falls apart with sheer implausibility, the plot predictable even before the end of the first half. Again Costner was singled out by *Variety* as the only decent thing about the film – as again were the excessive semi-porn aspects: '*Shadows Run Black* is notable only for its unusually capacious amount of full nudity featuring well-built young women, an obvious draw in the cassette market. Tech credits are weak and acting, apart from Costner, only semi-pro.'

Eric Louzil, the film producer responsible for the romps, recalled how he had to get Costner drunk to perform in one of the steamier love scenes in *Sizzle Beach, USA* with Leslie Brander. 'Kevin was very nervous about doing it,' said Louzil. 'We had to give him some wine. He was having a really hard time. We always laugh about that scene. He

Above: Costner in a scene from *Sizzle Beach, USA* with Leslie Brander, wife of the director, Richard Brander. Costner had to be loosened up with wine to get him through his first love scene with her. Right: The poster for *Sizzle Beach, USA*. He claimed it had 'tit or ass every six minutes but wasn't porn'.

Costner in his first role as 'stud' farmer John Logan in the Troma Films soft porn movie *Sizzle Beach, USA*.

had to make love to the director's wife in front of a fireplace. He kissed her, but it was like he wasn't into it.'

Nonetheless, Costner did acknowledge some good came out of his screen debut. 'The experience helped me,' he said. 'I suddenly knew what type of actor I really wanted to be – and acting became holy to me.' It's worth noting that Costner made a brief cameo appearance in another obscure film from that era, *Chasing Dreams*. Filmed in 1981, the baseball-themed movie was never released until Costner's success with *Bull Durham* and *Field Of Dreams* in 1989. Costner has reportedly sued Prism Entertainment for marketing the video by displaying a picture of

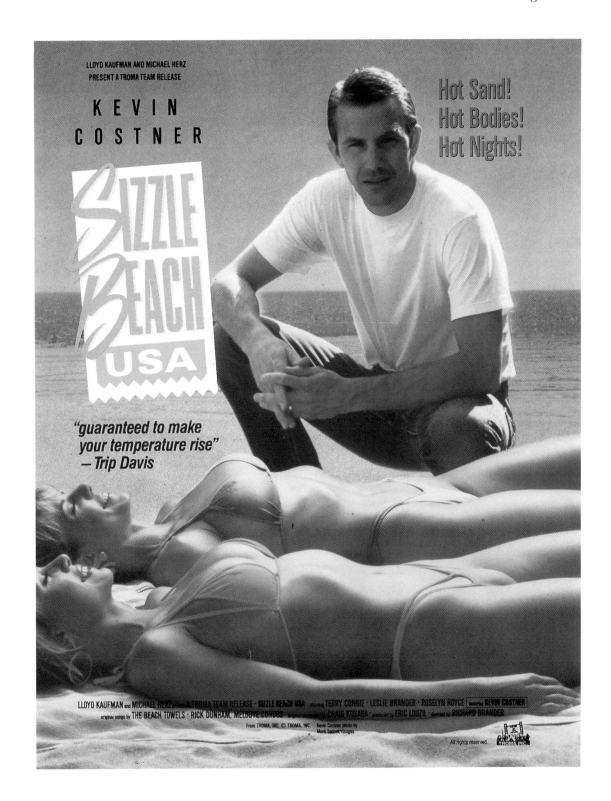

him on the cover in a baseball uniform, despite that fact that he is not seen playing the sport in the film. 'Production and most of cast is at best semi-pro,' wrote the reviewer in *Variety*. 'Costner's easygoing manner and delivery is as confident and developed here as in *Field Of Dreams*. Costner has more movie marginalia in his past than virtually any other contemporary star. In this one his role is limited to giving the hero (his younger brother) a pep talk in the opening scene on his way to medical school. Cast talks a lot about him but unfortunately for the filmakers Costner never shows up again.'

In spite, or maybe because of, these early Troma roles, Costner's problems were multiplying. The way his career was heading in 1981 made him wonder if he had one at all. In anguish, he considered his options. The main stumbling block was that he wasn't a member of the Screen Actors Guild of America. Without the SAG card he could not go after the kind of serious roles he wanted. To qualify for one, an actor had to have a speaking part in a union-recognised film. That seemed fair enough to Costner, but until then his movie credits had been strictly the non-union kind and most of his acting experience was in community theatre productions. Without contacts or an agent, most doors were closed to him. He was restless and impatient. In addition, his wife Cindy had been steadily growing tired of his single-minded ambition; friends have claimed that she had wanted him to give up acting, to take a 'real job' in a bank or something similar. Perhaps she felt her life was passing her by, that she wanted to start living again while she was still young enough to enjoy herself, instead of having to scrimp and save for the sake of Costner's faltering career. She was probably wishing they could start a family, but this was out of the question.

College friends were a constant reminder to Costner just how far short his financial life fell at that time. At get-togethers he forced himself to listen as they joyfully described new cars they had bought, their first homes, promotion at work. 'When they asked me what I was doing I said "I have an interview next month." They didn't understand,' he recalled. 'We'd [Cindy and he] have these long drives home at the end of the night, and I'd say, "What am I doing? I don't have a BMW. I don't have a lawn with dichondra." But I called myself an actor, and I knew that someday this would all happen.' Costner had felt guilty about the sacrifices his wife had made for him when he gave up his marketing career, but he would not give up his dream. 'In class there were moments when I felt like a monster – that strong. I felt I was that good in that moment! Making money was not the problem. Working was not the problem. What I didn't have was focus, a love of life.'

But just when things were looking really bad, Costner was given the chance to make a non-union picture called *Stacy's Knights*. As well as the welcome $500 per week pay packet, he would also meet the two men would later become an integral part of his climb to international stardom.

Shadows Run Black was another Troma low budget exploitation movie in which Costner starred as a thug suspected of a series of sex killings. Like *Sizzle Beach, USA* it would resurface again years later to cash in on the star's current stardom.

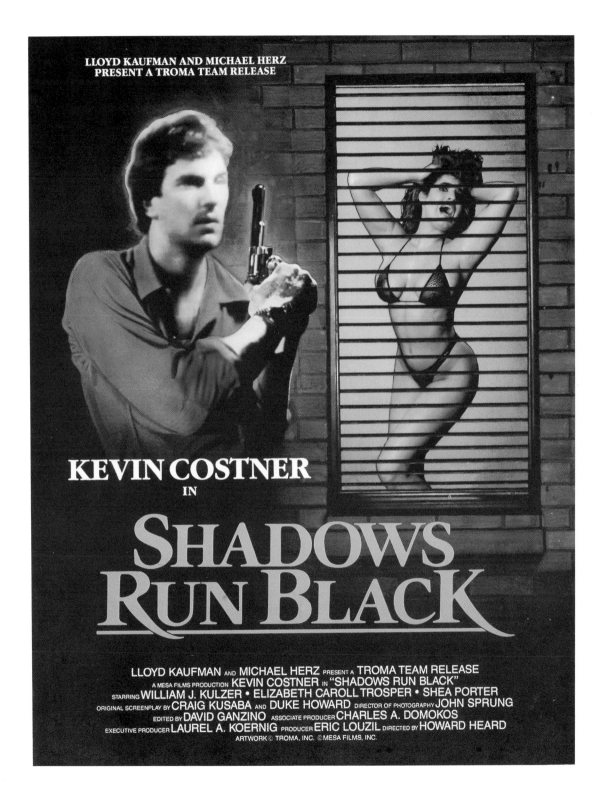

Chapter Two

No Way Out

HE was late. It was his first big audition and it now looked as if he would almost certainly miss it. He had taken the afternoon off from Raleigh Studios, but while driving his cheap, second-hand sedan along a freeway to the rehearsal venue on the other side of Hollywood, the car suddenly died. He could hardly believe it. Frantic, Costner flicked the ignition key, but the engine just spluttered again and stalled. He clambered out, looking around, cursing the car. Recalling the incident, he said: 'I left it, hopped a fence and hitch-hiked there.'

Showing the same kind of resourcefulness in a situation as his screen characters,

Kevin Costner as the happy-go-lucky gunslinger, Jake, in *Silverado* (1985), the film that really brought him to public notice for the first time.

Costner eventually reached the audition – and got the part. It was in a low budget gambling picture called *Stacy's Knights*, written by an aspiring young novelist called Michael Blake. The director was Jim Wilson, a graduate of the Berkeley Film Institute and founder of the small production company, American Twist Productions, which was making the movie – though up until that point he had only produced and directed short films for such commercial clients as Volvo and Kodak. Wilson, Blake and Costner forged an important bond on this first project which was eventually to blossom into something much bigger.

Jim Wilson has vivid memories of the day he first met Kevin Costner: 'I had gone to film school with Michael Blake a few years earlier in Berkeley, and hired him to write the screenplay. It was the first movie I directed and the first he actually got paid to write. It was also Kevin's first starring role. We'd met a lot of actors for the lead role of Will Bonner, and then Kevin showed up to audition... Michael and I and the casting director unanimously agreed that he was the character.'

Wilson continued: 'I don't know where his instincts come from. His upbringing certainly wasn't in the field. He wasn't very well read. He didn't get good grades at school, but he has that whole streetwise thing and some life experience behind him that a lot of these kids in the business who are very pampered and went to the right academies and prestigious colleges don't have. I don't think they have the same spine he had.'

Michael Blake recalled the day when he first set eyes on the good-looking young would-be actor. 'I came back from lunch and was parking my motorcycle when I saw this guy out of the corner of my eye walking up and down in front of the little theatre where we were auditioning the actors. He seemed so intense, so real. He looked like a kid who'd just finished basketball practice. But even then producers and casting directors saw the footage and said, "Hey, this guy could be a leading man."'

Costner could not believe his good fortune in landing the part, especially when it also offered the chance to go on location. 'I remember Jim [Wilson] had to make this big decision whether to rent me a big room by myself or make me room with somebody else. For someone to give me five hundred bucks to act, I felt like a giant.'

Set in Reno, Nevada, *Stacy's Knights* follows the adventures of a shy drama school student Stacy (Andra Millian) who happens also to be a cardsharp. She visits the world-renowned

Above: In *Stacy's Knights*, a gambling film set in Reno, Will (Costner) shows shy drama student Stacy (Andra Millar) round the world-renowned casinos.

casinos of Reno, accompanied by her teacher Jean (Eve Lilith), with one purpose in mind...to make a killing on the blackjack tables. There they meet Will (Costner), a local boy who promises to show them a good time. But as the film progresses, Will is soon revealed as a double-dealing opportunist;

then teaches Stacy the ancient, and secret art of counting in blackjack.

Surprisingly, Will is then removed from the film by the bad guys. But undeterred, and not so shy any more, Stacy decides to carry on with 'The Sting', recruiting more players in the process. To fool the casino staff, she slips into disguise, dressing as a man and wearing a false moustache and glasses, and runs off with over half-a-million dollars in winnings.

Unfortunately *Stacy's Knights* was a gamble that didn't pay off, an over-ambitious and chronically dated disaster, not helped by the inexperience of all involved. Critics dismissed it as 'no ace movie', 'a below average intelligence TV movie', and 'a stillborn feature mechanically directed by Wilson'.

But for Costner it was a 'learning experience'. The film may have been a failure, but he had been the leading man, and he had enjoyed being the centre of attention. Inspired, he carried on with his acting studies while at the same time continuing to look for other movie roles. Then, at the end of 1981 he tried some modelling but it wasn't a success. Photographer Barry McKinley shot him for the January 1982 cover of *GQ* magazine and paid him $75, but the pictures were pulled when an editorial decision was overruled in favour of Zubin Mehta, and they never appeared. Costner still cringes at the memory of that photo session, and has said that the pictures 'didn't even look like me. They kept sticking all this crap in my hair'.

For all his enthusiasm, offers of work at the start of 1982 were few and far between. Costner had registered as an extra at Francis Ford Coppola's Zoetrope Studios, but he had to wait several months for the opportunity to

having recognised Stacy's potential and amazing photographic memory, he suggests a scam whereby the trio can clean up at a casino owned by the local king-pin, Shecky Poole (Mike Reynolds).

Stacy is coached by Will, they become lovers, and the plan is set in motion. But Poole thwarts their actions when he orders his best blackjack dealer to get rid of Stacy by cheating. Fortunately, Will's father, a one-time famous cardsharp himself, takes Stacy and her aides, her 'Knights', to a mystic known simply as The Kid (Ed Semenza). He appear in another picture. A former casting director at Zoetrope, Jane Jenkins, recalled how 'Someone called and told me about this guy who was really nice and good-looking and said we should use him as an extra or something. So Kevin came over and he was a big tall guy who was good-looking and smart. So we put him in *Frances*.'

Frances was a film biography being made by Mel Brooks' company about the tragic life of the1940s movie star, Frances Farmer. Made in much the same mood as the team's earlier success *The Elephant Man,* the film starred Jessica Lange (as Farmer) and Sam Shepard. Costner was cast as the actor, Luther Adler.

Costner's working relationship with the director of *Frances*, Graeme Clifford, was abrasive and they clashed continually on the set. In a foretaste of the perfectionism (or arrogance as some would have it) for which he was later to become notorious, things came to a head when Costner refused to say what he regarded as an inappropriate line of dialogue in the film. He insisted that Luther Adler would not have said the words 'Good night, Frances' to Farmer as they left the theatre after a show. Costner's reasoning was that since they had come out of the stage door separately, it would have been 'out of character' for Adler to have said the words.

Several takes later, and after much bickering between Costner and Clifford, the actor eventually said his only sentence of dialogue in the film through clenched teeth. Perhaps not surprisingly, Costner's part was cut from the finished film, though he wasn't too disheartened as he had at last managed to obtain his SAG card, without which it was impossible for him to progress any further in Hollywood. 'It's a fact of life for a film actor, that when you do small parts, they are going to be first to go,' he said later.

Almost immediately after *Frances*, Costner landed another small role in Francis Ford Coppola's lavish musical extravaganza *One From The Heart*, starring Nastassia Kinski and Frederic Forrest – but once again all his scenes were removed from the final footage. Unperturbed, Costner signed up for Ron Howard's *Night Shift*. The television comedy actor, still trying to shake off the typecasting of 'Richie Cunningham' from *Happy Days*, was cutting his teeth as a director. The main stars in this likeable black comedy were Henry ('The Fonz') Winkler, Michael Keaton and Shelley Long (star of *Cheers*).

As the title suggests, *Night Shift* is all about working in the twilight hours. 'Graveyard Shift' might have been more appropriate as the main character, Chuck Lumley III (Winkler), works for the New York City Morgue, a job he takes after becoming disenchanted with his former life as a financial whizz-kid on Wall Street – and to escape from his nagging fiancée Charlotte (Gina Hecht). Shortly after he starts there, Lumley becomes friends with fast-talking, nonconformist Billy Blaze (Keaton)...and before long the enterprising pair are running a call-girl agency from the morgue, using Billy's ideas, Chuck's financial expertise, and the morgue's limousines. Costner's appearance is brief: in a cast list of 50-plus, he's way down the pecking order – eighth from the end – billed as '1st Frat Boy' in a brat-pack of six. The scene to watch out for is where the fraternity boys, led by Costner, try to raid the morgue.

After being in a movie set in a morgue, it was odd that Costner should be asked to play a corpse in the next: Lawrence Kasdan's cult movie *The Big Chill*. As Alex, the man whose suicide and funeral reunites his old college classmates, Costner was supposed to appear in flashback as the friends reminisce about him and re-evaluate their own lives over the twenty-year gap that has elapsed since they were all at college together. The cast assembled for the movie now reads like a Hollywood 'who's who': Tom Berenger, Glenn Close, Jeff Goldblum, William Hurt, Kevin Kline, Mary Kay Place, Meg Tilly, JoBeth Williams. It was thanks to a casting director

Below: Costner's small part in Ron Howard's *Night Shift* was one of the few in his early years which wasn't cut from the film.

called Wally Nicita, who had mentioned him to Kasdan a year earlier, that Costner found himself reading for the chance to be part of such an illustrious cast. 'Boy, was I nervous, and I'm not normally,' he recalled. 'I felt no personal accord with this guy, but I knew he mattered. He called me back four times, and each interview was more nerve-wracking.'

But as luck would have it, Kasdan was forced to cut Costner's role severely; apart from a brief glimpse in the coffin – his ten-minute scene had been left on the cutting-room floor. That left Kasdan with the equally distressing task of having to tell the enthusiastic novice. Just ten days before the film was released at cinemas, he made the call. According to Kasdan, Costner 'reacted amazingly well. I think he was unhappy, but the

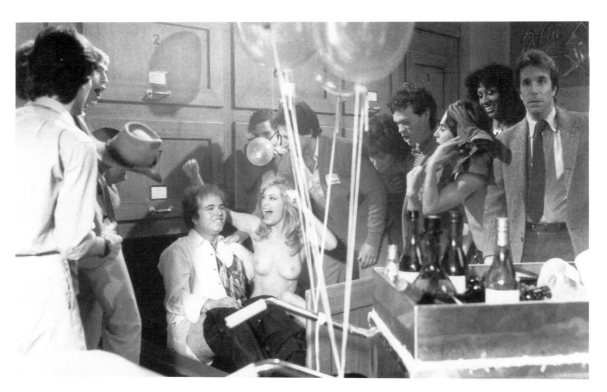

experience was so valuable to him that it didn't destroy him. I said, "It hurts me as much as it hurts you." And I said we'd do something again.'

As Costner has recalled of his conversation with Kasdan, 'He said, "How're you doing Kevin?" And before he spoke another word, I said, "You cut me out of the film, didn't you?" To say I wasn't mildly disappointed would not even be human, but during the making of the movie, I was very comfortable with being an actor and rehearsing and understanding what the work is all about.' Costner has admitted, with hindsight, cutting his character from *The Big Chill* had been the right decision. 'Cutting Alex out made the film play better. He was so unlikeable as written and in the flashback scenes I shot that you wonder why all these people would get together and mourn him.' But, he added: 'I could get cut out of a million movies, but getting cut out of a $100 million hit, that was something.'

It was also thanks to Wally Nicita's recommendation that Costner finally found an agent to represent him. Nicita had first met Costner when he came along to audition for a part in the 1981 Debra Winger movie *Mike's Murder*. Although he had failed to get the part, Nicita had been impressed enough to mention his name to her many showbusiness contacts. 'The kid just had it when he walked into that room. He has all the instincts of the greats,' she recalled. Nicita's assistant had been married to Gary Lucchesi, then an agent at the William Morris agency, so she called up Lucchesi and suggested he meet the promising young actor whom she regarded as 'star material'. Lucchesi was soon to leave the company to become an executive at Tri-Star,

but his colleague J.J. Harris had been happy to become Costner's agent. 'Kevin had self-confidence from the beginning,' Harris recollected. 'I'm sure he's had it forever. He's a bigger-than-life person whose presence fills a room, though not in an ostentatious way.'

The weight of the select William Morris agency behind him was reflected in the higher calibre of work Costner was now being offered. He had turned down the Matthew Broderick role in John Badham's *War Games* when *The Big Chill* had become available, against Harris's advice and after earlier accepting the part. A recurring facet of Costner's career, he has consistently made bad choices: he turned down the Jeff Bridges part in *Jagged Edge*, the Mel Gibson part in *Mrs Soffel*, the Willem Dafoe role in *Mississippi Burning*, Alec Baldwin's in *The Hunt For Red October*, and Tom Berenger's in the Oscar-winning Oliver Stone film *Platoon*.

In fact it was because of the similar experiences suffered by his brother Dan, a Vietnam veteran, that Costner baulked at the latter. 'I didn't want to get involved in a film about something that had such a traumatic impact on my brother's life,' he later explained. 'He's had such a problem with Vietnam movies that have shown vets as wigged-out guys. He's very proud that he came back and made a life for himself, that he went to college and has a family. And when I read *Platoon*, the murder theme just jumped out at me so much that I thought, I can't do this to him. But maybe, in retrospect, I should have tried to be in the movie. In fact, *Platoon* was real and it was right.' Similarly, Costner did not want to get involved with *The Ice Pirates*, *Grandview USA* and – with good sense, as it would later prove – the Madonna-Sean Penn fiasco *Shanghai Surprise*. But he has also lost out on films he did want desperately to be in, namely *The Killing Fields*, *Mask*, and the Nicolas Cage role in *Raising Arizona*.

The disappointment of *The Big Chill* behind him now, Costner went straight into shooting the holocaust drama, *Testament*, which he described as 'this little thing – with a budget of under a million dollars – for Public Broadcasting which attracted my attention'. The casting director for the TV film, Margery Simkin, was another person who noticed Costner's personal magnetism. She said: 'I was auditioning people in a big building where there were a lot of secretaries. And Kevin was just sitting in the waiting room wearing jeans and looking like he hadn't shaved – he just looked like a schlump. But after he left, every woman in that waiting area, and every secretary came in and said, "Who was that guy?!" I've never seen anything quite like it; they just went crazy over him. It's probably the only time I can think of where that happened. I was never surprised that he became a star.'

Testament was about the aftermath of a nuclear attack. Costner was enthusiastic about the project: 'I couldn't play the lead role because Jane Alexander did, but could I have donned a wig, I really would have!' Similar in subject to a rival and much more successful TV movie at that time, *The Day After*, events focus on a small, out-of-the-way Californian town plunged into a catastrophe of nightmarish proportions when missiles rain down on the surrounding area without any warning. Although not a direct hit of the surprise attack on the U.S. (the town's position – sheltered by a mountain ridge – has helped save it from the blast) a power failure

ensures that maximum panic and confusion follows. Bewildered at first, the plucky community take measures to ration food and petrol as they decide what to do next.

A little hope is hinted at when an amateur radio enthusiast (played by Leon Ames) manages to contact other cities, but to everyone's growing desperation finds that the rest of the country is just as much in the dark as they are, and can offer no real clue to the cause of the devastation. Central characters are the Wetherly family: Dad (William Devane) is stuck in San Francisco at the time and is unable to get back home, while Mother (Jane Alexander) and their three children gradually fall victim to radiation sickness, and impending death. Costner and Rebecca De Mornay play Phil and Cathy Pitkin, other sorry casualties of the silent, invisible war, who drive off in search of 'a safe place' after their baby dies.

Slowly building to a numbing climax, *Testament*'s strength lies in its simple, unwavering chronicle of the despair and degradation suffered by ordinary people – whom the audience are made to feel, quite unequivocally, could just as easily be them – as their lives, hopes and aspirations are shattered by the sheer futility of the senseless waste. Critics described *Testament* as 'tremendously moving' and 'exceptionally powerful' and Costner felt justifiably proud of the warm reception the film received. 'I sensed I was a part of something really great from the beginning and a year later when *Testament* came out, we realised how really wonderful it was. And,' he added, 'there was also a bit of interest in me!'

After the sombre mood of *Testament*, Costner flew to Greece for his next assign-

In *Testament*, a made-for-TV drama about the nuclear holocaust, Kevin Costner and Rebecca De Mornay played Phil and Cathy Pitkin, the young parents whose baby is dying of radiation sickness.

ment in *Table For Five*, a Jon Voight movie being made mostly on location onboard the *S.S. Vistafjord* which was actually making a cruise at the time from Rome to Athens and then on to Cairo. With steady offers of film

work coming in, Costner felt confident enough to resign from his job at Raleigh Studios after more than three years there. Costner was cast as one of the 'newlyweds' with Cynthia Kania as his wife. The actors had all been given their own cabins on the luxury cruiser; on the days they weren't actually involved with filming, they took advantage of the facilities available on board: the large, tiered swimming pool, table tennis and raquetball courts, sunbeds on the forward deck...willing extras, mixing with the real, fare-paying holidaymakers, adding authenticity to the scenes.

Table For Five was clearly a vehicle for Voight. With the success of *The Champ* four years earlier, filmmakers were eager to develop the parental side of the star; instead of one child, however, he was now the father of three. As divorced husband J. P. Tannen, Voight comes to reclaim the children from his ex-wife Kathleen (Millie Perkins) and her new husband Mitchell (Richard Crenna), after ignoring the children for several years. To make up for his neglect, Tannen takes them on a fantastic voyage through the Mediterranean. While at sea, his ex-wife is tragically killed in a car accident and her husband comes to collect the children. Thus begins a custody battle between the fathers, with the moral issue of natural parents versus adoptive parents becoming the crutch of the slow-moving, sentimental drama.

As the newlyweds, Costner and Kania had little more to do than glue to each other, smiling constantly against the backdrop of the beautiful travelogue scenery. In the end, Costner, who had become known in the business as 'The Face On The Cutting Room Floor', was depressed but unsurprised to learn that most of his scenes had been cut from the story.

By this stage in his career in 1983, Costner was growing increasingly frustrated. He seemed to be going nowhere. Perhaps his expectations were too high, and he was meant to be stuck in supporting roles for the rest of his career. As the veteran actor told the novice in popular Hollywood legend: 'Casting directors are up to their ass in the next Jimmy Stewart/Gregory Peck/Robert Mitchum. Everybody wants to be a chief, nobody wants to be an Indian. Take my advice and lower your sights. It's still acting, the work's regular, and the money ain't too bad – and at least you'll have peace of mind.'

But peace of mind wasn't compensation enough for a nondescript career, and Costner nagged his agent for more important roles. After the countless bit-parts since *Stacy's Knights*, Costner finally landed his first real leading role in *The Gunrunner*, a Canadian production originally entitled *St. Louis Square*. It was not the kind of quality role he had hoped for. A ludicrous film like *Sizzle Beach, USA* and *Shadows Run Black*, *The Gunrunner* would also turn up on video (six years later, in 1989) to capitalize on Costner's stardom. And like its predecessors, Costner would disown it, this time claiming that as far as he was aware the film had been abandoned before completion.

Costner plays the gunrunner, Ted Beaubien, an illegal arms dealer caught up in the dark and supposedly menacing underworld of 1926 Montreal. All the clichés of gangster movies are thrown in, with Beaubien's reckless younger brother George (Ron Lea) getting himself killed while trying to set up a deal to purchase weapons, George's girlfriend Rosalyn (Mitch Martin) being kidnapped and held to ransom for the gun money, and Beaubien being left to sort out the sorry mess while at the same time battling constantly with his strong-willed, whisky-swigging girlfriend Maude (Sara Botsford), who just happens to own a speakeasy of ill-repute. Looking like the hastily put together package it is, the end result is a confusing muddle with little or no imagination and even less action or suspense. When it finally came out on video, the film received the reviews it deserved. Typical is *Variety*'s comment: 'A very dull show...an almost actionless vehicle that plays like a subpar telefilm.' It was hardly surprising that Costner would want to wash his hands of it later. 'I had decided by then, that come what may, I was going to hold out for better roles,' he said.

Kevin Costner had to delay until the following year for his next role, but he felt it was worth waiting for. He was overjoyed when an unknown director named Kevin Reynolds hired him for a starring role in the comedy *Fandango*. The film was being produced by Amblin Entertainments, Steven Spielberg's production company, so Costner had high hopes for the quality of the project.

Costner soon found out that it wasn't the first time he had come across *Fandango*, or Kevin Reynolds for that matter. 'When I was stage-managing I would always look for little plays or student films or whatever I could do after work,' he said. 'And I went to read for a student film, a short version of *Fandango*, to be made by this young director Kevin Reyolds. It got right down to me and another actor and of course I didn't get the part...Three years later, I wander into this office for an audition for another film, called *Fandango*, and it was the same one!'

The latest in a long line of nostalgic coming-of-age movies spawned from the success of *American Graffiti* eleven years earlier (such as *National Lampoon's Animal House* and *Porky's*), *Fandango* focuses on a group of college boys who go on a pre-Vietnam fling to Mexico in 1971. Opening at a fraternity party in the boys' home town of Austin, Texas, Kenneth Waggener (Sam Robards) announces that he has called off his wedding because he has been drafted. His best friend, magnetic and manipulative Gardner Barnes (Costner) is quick to suggest that they celebrate their last weekend of freedom as all true American boys should: chasing girls, having a good time and plenty to drink. Gardner then recruits Phil Hicks (Judd Nelson) who has the all important automobile, Dorman (Chuck Bush) and Lester (Brian Cesak), and together the group – known collectively as 'The Groovers' – break for the border in order to 'dig up Dom' (fraternity slang for their favourite drink, Dom Perignon champagne).

But the Groovers' plans are temporarily waylaid when Phil's car runs out of petrol in the desert. They somehow manage to make it to a small town where they 'make out' with two young girls, Judy and Lorna (Elizabeth Daily and Robyn Rose), dubbed 'jailbait' by them because of their age. Forced to spend the night in the town while the car is being repaired, they are taken by the girls to the local graveyard for a fireworks fight. This experience brings home to Gardner and Waggener what it will be like in Vietnam, and the possibility that they may die there. Gardner announces that he is going to dodge the draft, and Waggener sides with him. But Phil – who's vehemently patriotic and already enlisted in the army – tries to coax Waggener out of it. He confronts Gardner. This leads to conflict between the friends until Phil makes a near-fatal parachute jump at a parachute

Costner was almost 30 when he was cast as an 'eternal student' in the coming-of-age college movie *Fandango* to explain away his maturing looks.

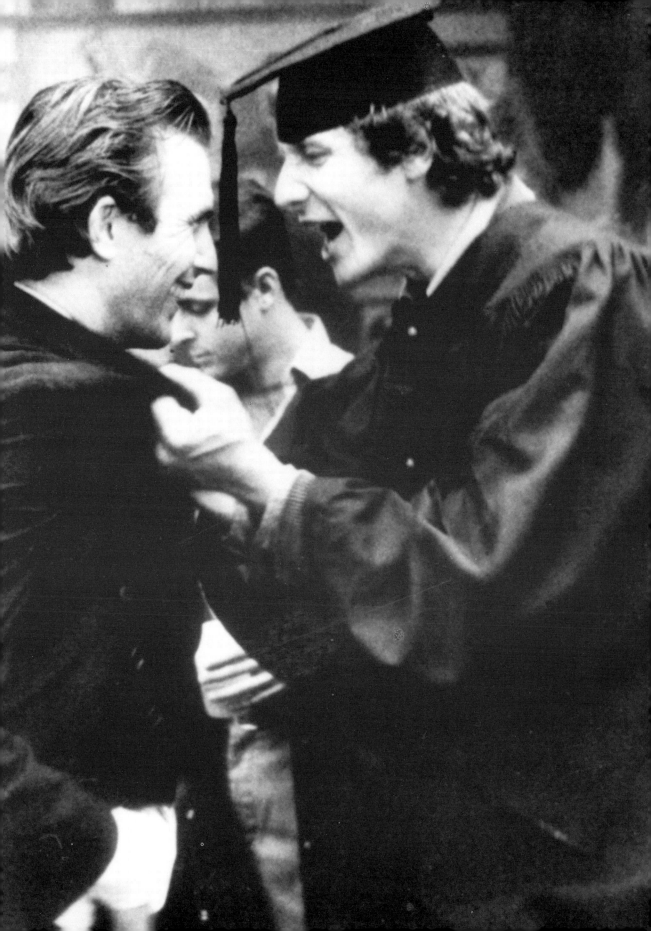

school in the desert to prove his point. Having faced death, Phil is reconciled with Gardner and Waggener, and Waggener decides he does want to get married after all. After the hastily arranged ceremony, the Groovers break up.

With Spielberg's company overseeing the venture, Costner felt confident about the film's chances. Indeed when it was premiered at the Venice Film Festival in 1985, *Fandango* was accorded standing ovations, but when it was released in America shortly afterwards, it failed to gross more than $2 million. Costner was nonetheless grateful for the experience. 'It changed my whole outlook. It's a mixed bag but ultimately it was a really good little movie, one of my favourites.' *Variety* was full of praise for his performance. 'Costner is a dynamic presence at the film's centre,' wrote its reviewer. 'Charismatic enough to hold both the fictional group and the pic together, he has the sort of dangerous unpredictability that makes for top flight performers. The others are not in his league but are up to the demands placed upon them.' Irma Velasco in *People* agreed: 'Costner does seem as if he could talk a riled-up rattler out of his fangs.'

After the failure of *Fandango*, Costner plunged straight into John Badham's cycle race movie *American Flyers*. Costner was relieved to see that the director had forgiven him for earlier pulling out of *War Games*. A tale of sibling rivalry in the saddle, he was to play one half of the battling Sommers brothers, rivals in what was supposed to be the most dangerous and gruelling bike race in the world – the infamous 'Hell of the West'. Costner trained intensely for the role, peddling around the streets of Los Angeles, building up his stamina and learning about

Above: Costner in his backyard reading the script for *American Flyers*. While he has never claimed to 'work out' to maintain body fitness, his natural athleticism has kept him trim over the years.

gear changes and race tactics; a perfectionist, he was determined to look convincing in the part. In one scene where he is seen riding at speed, Costner shows his confidence by unwrapping and eating a bar of chocolate with both hands off the handlebars; later he has a water bottle fight on the bikes with co-star David Grant.

These newly acquired riding skills would come in useful later in 1985 when he attended the Venice Film Festival for the screenings of *Fandango* and *Silverado*. One evening he and Mel Gibson got drunk in the Excelsior bar. The Australian actor had become so enthusiastic after hearing Costner's stories about the making of *American Flyers*, that he had suggested they go for a spin on some bicycles he had seen earlier on his way to the bar. As Costner remembered it, 'We went outside, and they were all locked. So Mel went off and found one, but not two. I said I'd ride; I'd just done this bike picture. And it was great. There we were, on the Lido, and Mel's on the goddamned handlebars looking like E.T.!'

Steve Tesich, who wrote the screenplay for *American Flyers*, recalled his first ride with Costner at Griffith Park – where, 30 years earlier, James Dean and Dennis Hopper clashed in the famous clifftop scene in *Rebel Without A Cause*. Fast approaching that same hill, Tesich felt the athletic actor beginning to pick the pace up ever so slightly. Suddenly, and without any warning, Costner kicked out with everything he had, his bike surging forward ahead of the more experienced rider. Breathing quickly, Tesich had followed in hot pursuit. According to the writer, Costner 'really wanted to beat me. This was no small inner desire, but really out front. I wanted to

be on top. I had to beat him, and I did. Why? It was my sport...and my script!'

For the Hell of the West race, hundreds swarm to Colorado to compete, but only the fittest, strongest and bravest riders stand any chance of finishing, let alone winning. Marcus Sommers (Costner) is a serious-minded sports doctor, a fading rider with one great race left in him. His younger brother David (David Grant) is a dreamer who has side-stepped his responsibilities for most of his life, to Marcus' unbridled resentment. Formerly estranged, but now reunited after the tragic death of their father, both live with the fear that they may have inherited the hereditary disease (cerebral aneurysm) which killed him. And both enter the race believing that it could very well be their last.

As the race progresses, the brothers untangle their mixed emotions and resolve to sort out their differences before it's too late. They are joined en route by Marcus' girl-friend Sarah (Rae Dawn Chong) and a hitch-hiker, Becky (Alexandra Paul), who becomes David's girlfriend. In the face of insuperable odds, and with the girls cheering on fanatically from the side-lines, combativeness between brothers eventually gives way to camaraderie.

American Flyers was unfortunately another film hampered by clichés, and full of stereotype characters, such as a hulking blond Russian champion, whose use of steroids and bad sportsmanship to better his chances only served to make the outcome all the more inevitable. The late Leslie Halliwell, precise and to the point as always, described it in his indispensable filmgoers handbook as an 'Ambitious but ineffective drama with too much effort to explore personal dramas instead of getting on with the action.' *Variety* was equally dismissive for much the same reasons: 'This overblown production just pumps hot air in too many directions and comes up limp.'

Some critics were more optimistic of the film's chances. *American Flyers* was released after *Silverado,* although shot beforehand, and Costner had begun to make his mark in the latter film when reviewers were assessing *American Flyers.* For instance, David Ansen wrote in *Newsweek*: 'It's tempting to dismiss *American Flyers* as the most shamelessly manipulative movie of the season. It combines two of the wettest ploys of the era: the win-one-for-the-gipper athletic competition (in this case bicycle racing) and the hereditary-disease-strikes-down-youth gambit. The exasperating thing is that writer Steve Tesich and director John Badham are no hacks: the details and dialogue are consistently superior to the sappy themes. So is the quietly powerful Costner, who proves that his *Silverado* flash was not in the pan.'

The break for Costner finally came when Lawrence Kasdan kept his promise to make up for cutting him out of *The Big Chill.* Kasdan created the role of gunslinger Jake with Costner in mind. He wanted Costner in the film because 'he has energy, lightness, speed, and, at the same time, intensity. I wanted the Jake character to have that kind of untamed energy, the reckless, forward movement that always attracted me to Westerns.'

As with *The Big Chill,* Kasdan had again assembled an impressive cast that included Kevin Kline, Rosanna Arquette, Jeff Goldblum, Brian Dennehy, Scott Glen, Danny Glover, Linda Hunt and British comedy actor John Cleese (star of the British television

American Flyers (1985). Always the perfectionist, Costner (with David Grant) was determined to look good in the race sequences and trained intensely for the role.

series *Monty Python's Flying Circus* and *Fawlty Towers,* who would later achieve a cult following in America for his portrayal of a bumbling barrister in *A Fish Called Wanda*). Cleese's brief appearance as a pragmatic English sheriff brought a fine edge to a film already laced with quirky humour. 'Cleese was great,' Costner said. 'The minute we all put on our guns, we behaved like children and started chasing each other around. There wasn't an adult to be found. *Silverado* has everything you might imagine. To be on horses, to be with a bunch of guys and to shoot guns. It was great fun.'

In addition to learning the necessary sharp-shooting skills, compulsory riding lessons daily lasting a month were also imposed on the stars. Costner in particular relished the fast-action riding scenes, with his ruthless determination to perform his own stunts surfacing for the first time as he learned to leap out of a window onto the saddle of a horse. Early in the film he is seen clambering over the cell in the town jail, swinging like a monkey from bar to bar in the iron cage. Costner admitted that refusing to have a stunt double was his big chance to make an impression in the film: 'These were chances I didn't want to turn over to someone else.' And as his reckless character Jake would be called on to perform some quite exaggerated feats of bravado towards the end of the movie, he defended the risks he had taken by insisting that he had to 'put

in a lot of high-voltage action early on to make it credible – or acceptable anyway'. Stephen Schiff commented in *Vanity Fair*: 'Just standing and delivering his lines, Costner projects a fascinating volatility. You don't know what he might do next: grab the gun, grab the girl, or do a back-flip. He is something the movies haven't seen for a while...a leading man.'

The story is set in the 1880s. Emmett (Scott Glen), a wronged killer newly released from jail, is riding to Silverado to rejoin his family. Along the way, he's ambushed by gunmen, he kills them, then rescues Paden (Kevin Kline), a man the gunmen had earlier left to die in the desert. The two team up and head for the stop off town of Turley where Emmett is to meet his younger brother Jake (Costner). On their arrival they witness a noisy commotion in the saloon, where a black man, Mal (Danny Glover), has been refused a drink. They speak up for him, but Sheriff Langston (Cleese) steps in and orders Mal to leave town. Then they hear that a hanging is about to take place, but to his alarm, Emmett discovers that it is Jake – a wild, reckless, womaniser – who is to be

Director Lawrence Kasdan (far right) confers on set with the cast of *Silverado* (left to right: Danny Glover, Kevin Kline, Scott Glenn and Kevin Costner). By casting him, in this movie, Kasdan repaid Costner for cutting his scenes from *The Big Chill*.

strung up. Later, Langston throws Paden in jail for killing a man in self-defence, and he looks set for the same fate as Jake. However, Emmett breaks them out and with the help of Mal, who later appears with his deadly accurate rifle, they manage to escape Langston and his posse. While making tracks for Silverado, they stumble upon settlers who tell them about the ruthless land baron McKendrick (Ray Baker) whose men are robbing everyone heading there to prevent them making claims on land he wants. The foursome decide to take on the McKendrick clan, and right the wrongs.

Silverado is a formula Western, bordering

Costner shows off his sharp-shooting skills in a scene from *Silverado* with Kevin Kline, right. Costner said working on the movie was 'great fun'.

almost on parody, with every cowboy scene you've ever seen and loved thrown in quite unashamedly – from the 'High Noon' shoot-outs, the cattle stampedes, the dusty trails, to the saloon bar brawls, the settler's pretty widow, the ruthless and powerful villain and the Magnificent Four riding to the rescue of those being persecuted by him. Richard

Corliss in *Time* wrote: 'Now there's *Silverado*, the Cuisinart western! *Silverado* dices, splices, chops, co-opts, hones and clones every oater archetype in just 2 hr 13 min; that's less than 1% of the time it would take you to sit through the collected works of John Wayne! Lawrence Kasdan has performed deft surgery on the Saturday-matinee serial and the film noir melodrama. But the western will not yield.' *Variety* deemed the film to be 'less like the film Westerns of imagination and more like something more common. Maybe it was that way in real life'. Its reviewer continued: '*Silverado* is an entertaining but not totally satisfying attempt to revive the Western genre. While there is much to applaud Lawrence Kasdan's elaborate production, his modern reworking of mythical themes results in a kind of hybrid form.'

Costner disagreed with the reviews. He argued that Jake, who was certainly the most colourful of the four cowboys, was a character rarely seen in a Western before: a headstrong, troublesome sort whom he described as being 'quite dangerous'. He went on to explain how Jake was more of a hindrance than a help to his friends. 'He's a character that will certainly get killed, or at worst get someone that you like in the film killed.'

Costner has likened his experience on *Silverado* to *The Big Chill*. 'Again it was the right film, the right group, the right time,' he said. It also gave him another opportunity to work with Kevin Kline and Jeff Goldblum from the earlier film. 'A Kasdan film is like being part of a family,' he said.

He claimed that it had only needed someone like Kasdan to give him his big break. 'I knew it'd take just one powerful person to like me and I'd be on my way, but a lot of powerful people are wimps. I didn't go to parties to shake their hands. I waited for them to come to me.' And they did. For the first time Costner had become noticed and other directors were beginning to express an interest in working with him. Whether he liked it or not, he had attracted a buzz.

Kevin Costner insisted on doing his own stunts in *Silverado* in order as he put it 'to make an impression in the film'. It was a principle he continued into stardom, much to the consternation of his backers.

Chapter Three

Untouchable

AFTER the success of *Silverado*, Costner's agent began to be inundated with offers. In just six years, the star's pay cheque had jumped from $500 for *Sizzle Beach, USA*, to $500,000 in 1986 for his next film, *No Way Out*. It also brought the chance to become one of the hottest leading men in Hollywood, an expectation shared by the producer of *No Way Out*, Laura Ziskin: 'There was a time when there was Redford, McQueen and Eastwood and now there's only Harrison Ford – and Kevin Costner.'

During this period, Costner was still living in a normal middle class residential neigh-

Kevin Costner as Eliot Ness in the climax of *The Untouchables*, the film that made him a star. Film critic Pauline Kael praised him for being 'the essence of laid back'.

bourhood, an ordinary guy among ordinary people. At first the novelty of stardom was a cause of wonder to him. On location in Washington D.C. the studio booked its star into a $1,000-a-night hotel suite. The hotel, near the capital's Dulles airport, was utterly luxurious. A bell-boy had led Costner into the beautiful drawing room, done in soft pastel shades, furnished with plush couches and armchairs, antique tables and its own bar stocked with drinks. A connecting door revealed an equally impressive master-bedroom with an oversized bed and Impressionist paintings on the wall. Feeling awkward and embarrassed, Costner had been unsure how much he should tip the boy and had waited until he had left before wandering back through the rooms again. Costner had been taken aback by these lavish surroundings. 'Every time they book me into one of these rooms I feel there must have been some mistake,' he said.

Costner had never travelled in a limousine until he was 28. When the first one appeared outside his Hollywood home he asked his neighbours to take a photograph of him standing next to it. 'You shouldn't ever take these luxury things for granted,' he told them. And Costner has made it clear that his head has not been turned by these temptations, something he credits to his strict upbringing. 'All the Costners are good men, my father would tell us. He said we should always keep in mind what's fluff and what's real.'

No Way Out was a classy re-make of the 1948 Ray Milland/Charles Laughton *film noir* classic *The Big Clock*. Instead of the publishing business, however, the action takes place in and around the Pentagon. Costner plays Lt. Commander Tom Farrell, a naval officer invited to a reception in Washington by his old friend Scott Pritchard (Will Patten). Introduced to but ignored by Scott's boss, Secretary of Defence David Brice (played by Gene Hackman), Tom soon finds himself in the arms of beautiful 'party' girl Susan Atwell (Sean Young). Both bored, they slip out together and thus begins a tempestuous affair between the two.

Returning to sea and becoming a hero after saving a crewman's life, Tom is seconded to the Department of Defence in recognition of his bravery. Working directly under Brice, his duties, he finds, are mainly to liaise with the CIA. But continuing where he left off in his romance with Susan, he becomes angry when she confesses she is the mistress of the devious Brice. Tom gives her an ultimatum: him or me. Susan resolves to leave Brice, but when she tries tell him their

affair is over he is consumed with jealousy and hits her, accidentally sending her over the bannister and to her death on the floor below. Panicking because someone saw him arrive at Susan's flat, he calls his assistant and close friend Scott, a homosexual in love with Brice, who uses his subversive contacts to cover up the death. The next morning, Tom is summoned into Brice's office and given a top secret mission: he has 48 hours to find the sole witness and prime suspect for the murder. But Tom is that witness, and he is the only person who can identify the killer.

Tom's mission becomes a frantic race against time as he gets tangled up in the intricate web of lies, counter bluffs and conspiracy in the corridors of power. As he tries to prevent the evidence pointing back to himself, inexorably the trap closes in on him even more. *No Way Out* was a tense, pacy thriller with clear sub-Watergate overtones and a neat, unexpected twist at the end. 'You're not going to know where this movie goes,' Costner said shortly before the film opened. 'I've always enjoyed stories where you think you've got everything figured out – then they spring the trap.' So unexpected was the trap that the presskit provide by the film's distributors, Orion Pictures, had asked reviewers not to reveal the final twist that Farrell was all the time a double-agent working for Soviet intelligence.

No Way Out, produced before *The*

In this exciting chase sequence in *No Way Out*, the 1986 remake of the 1948 movie *The Big Clock*, Farrell (Costner) weaves his way across a busy highway in a desperate attempt to distance himself from his pursuers.

Untouchables in 1986, was held back until the following year to benefit from the attention given to the big budget gangster movie. In the light of the Oliver North/Irangate scandal which surfaced at that time, this darker role of Costner's as a US naval officer/Russian spy embroiled in espionage made *No Way Out* a timely thriller in 1987. Critics, however, did not take kindly to the trick ending. 'The final flaw in *No Way Out* (a preposterous plot twist) spoils this lively, intelligent remake,' wrote Richard Schickel in *Time*. 'Why [director] Donaldson and writer Robert Garland chose to sacrifice

Kevin Costner with Sean Young in *No Way Out*. Below: Costner grapples with Gene Hackman in a scene from *No Way Out*.

sympathy for Costner's character (and their well-made movie) by giving him a second, superfluous identity is a mystery infinitely more baffling than the one they have made.' *The National Review*'s John Simon complained that the ending 'lacks a shred of sense and vitiates whatever credibility and sympathy may have been elicited before. That audiences are willing to sit through this ending without demanding their money back is perhaps even more astounding than a sudden discussion of Russian literature in an otherwise totally anti-intellectual context.' Simon, who obviously had difficulty liking movies that the public flocked to see, continued his review with a scalding attack on Costner's performance. 'Kevin Costner, the new superstar in the making, struck me as all right as the wild kid brother in the dreadful *Silverado*, and stiff and dullish as Eliot Ness in De Palma's unspeakable *Untouchables*. As Tom Farrell, he leaves me cold again: I don't trust a face with twice as much jaw to it as forehead, and though a gravelly voice can be interesting, a sandy one merely grates. Costner manages somehow to be both loutish and drab – but that may well be what this age craves in its heroes.' Pauline Kael in *The New Yorker* was surprisingly more respectful: 'As an eagerly rising young man, Costner has a pleasant air of not thinking too much of himself, and he gives you the impression that he's doing what's wanted of him. Still, this agile fellow who spends the whole movie in movement is the essence of laid back. He has no inner energy.'

Costner has tried to explain the complexity of his character: 'Farrell is not always what he seems to be. He has three separate personalities: a professional one, a personal one and a private one, and until they finally collide and result in a real emotional outburst, the situation he's in at any given time determines what personality is up-front.'

He went on to draw parallels with his own personality: 'I believe I also have a facade – a rougher, tougher exterior. Also, like Farrell, there's a certain part of me that's cynical, a part that doesn't like authority. I can work within the framework of authority, but don't push me too far.'

The most talked about scene (and the best remembered) in *No Way Out* was Costner's steamy love scene with Sean Young in the back of a limousine as they cruised around the streets of Washington. The scene leaves nothing to the imagination – Costner and Young rip each other's clothes off as a grinning Costner tells the wide-eyed chauffeur watching them to wind up the blackened-out slide window, shutting off the driver's view in the mirror. Although Costner appears quite cocky and comfortable as he takes control of the situation, Sean Young claimed that her co-star had been very nervous before filming the scene. 'Kevin is a very shy man and he finds love scenes difficult,' she said. 'I knew he was worried about the limousine scene but on the day he was really shaking. I had to take charge of the situation. I cracked jokes, told him to take deep breaths and relax. I said, "I won't bite you", but I did. It was in the script!' She added: 'I think Kevin's got a deep puritanical streak in him. It was a very difficult scene to do. I was the vulnerable one. I was naked. He was extremely nervous, even terrified. I kept a poll of how many cast and crew members had screwed in cars. As it turned out I was the only one who hadn't done it before!'

Costner, who once said 'I'm more comfortable crashing onto a car windshield than I am in the back seat', tried to explain his apprehensions: 'I'd seen scenes like that done well and done badly. I didn't want to do it badly. I didn't want people to laugh at me. I've never watched anybody make love, so how do you know if you are doing it right?'

He continued: 'We're all red-blooded dudes. Someone takes her clothes off, I mean, there is a point where you have to look. But we had to be real hungry, and Sean understood that. But I had no feelings whether it was intense at all.'

His dashing portrayal of the handsome, clean-cut 'officer and gentleman' established Costner as Hollywood's hottest sex symbol, toppling Harrison Ford to become America's most desired action man. It also brought 500 marriage proposals every week from female fans. 'I personally don't think I'm that sexy,' Costner stated. 'I see guys that I think are classically handsome and know why a woman likes them. But I don't see myself that way. I can't live up to the media's expectations. I can't and won't be dictated to by what they say.'

Costner's former student friends at California State University at Fullerton asked him to host a benefit. As well as a sumptuous buffet, the $50 entrance fee included a sneak preview of *No Way Out* before it had gone on general release. Costner was also voted Star of Tomorrow by the National Association of Theatre Owners in America that year, but he could not collect his award as he was filming *The Untouchables*.

Repeating the role made famous by Robert Stack in the TV series *The Untouchables* – which ran from 1959 to 1964 in America –

Brian De Palma directing Kevin Costner on the set of *The Untouchables*. Costner's straightforward 'guy next door' image fitted De Palma's vision of Eliot Ness as a family man with a wife and young child to worry about.

Costner's asking price for playing the legendary crime-buster Eliot Ness had now risen to $800,000. With director Brian De Palma at the helm of the $14 million gangster epic, Costner's co-stars were to be Sean Connery, Robert De Niro and another rising young actor, Andy Garcia.

If Costner was nervous of the (female) Sean in his previous movie, this was equalled only by the apprehension he felt before meeting the (male) Sean in this one, though for very different reasons. Costner admitted that he had been in awe of the much-celebrated Scottish actor: 'I've always adored him from a distance. The reality of *The Untouchables* was that Sean was the star. I couldn't compete with that at the time and didn't try to. I appreciate both his professional and personal style – and try and learn from it.'

Andy Garcia added: 'When I was told I was being cast opposite him, I was really excited, and kinda nervous, too. People forget just how many films Connery's made, apart from all the James Bonds. But he made it easy for me, was really relaxing to work with, and I learned a lot just from being around the guy.'

'We determined beforehand that I was going to take them – onstage and offstage – under my wing,' Connery explained. Kevin Costner enjoyed Connery's company immensely. 'I really like to work with the best people possible,' he said.

One incident during a shooting break revealed Costner's ignorance of Connery's background and personal life, and a significant lack of knowledge of cinema history. Costner, who had an irritating habit of acting out scenes from his favourite films ('Do you know that he can do every scene from *How The West Was Won*?,' Costner's co-star in *Bull Durham*, Susan Sarandon, said wearily,) had taken it upon himself to entertain the cast with an improvised rendition of the Paul Newman/Richard Boone Western *Hombre*. His high-pitched rendition of the tough pioneer woman in the film was received with laughter. Turning to Connery at that point, Costner had asked him 'Who was that woman, anyway?' 'That was my wife?' answered Connery coldly. Costner had the grace to be embarrassed – the pioneer woman had been played by Diane Cilento, whom Conner had divorced many years previously. However Sean Connery soon put Costner at his ease.

Taking his research to almost method-acting extremes to get into the part of Ness, Costner devoured every book he could find on prohibition Chicago, the 'Roaring Twenties' and the mobster Ness finally brought to justice – Al Capone. He also interviewed the U.S. Treasury Department, FBI officers and people who had known the real Eliot Ness –

Eliot Ness (Costner) leads an ambush against the mob, backed up by tough veteran cop Jim Malone (Sean Connery).

including the sole surviving member of the 'Untouchables', Al Wolff, who was 85 years old at the time. Director Brian De Palma described the kind of help Wolff gave Costner: 'Al was very matter-of-fact. He gave Costner some useful insights into the character of Ness, who apparently was a quiet, methodical man.'

But, De Palma added: 'Ness states at the beginning of the film that he's going to get his man. He does get him, but in the process he loses his innocence and some of his best friends.'

According to Costner, his weeks of research 'went out the window when I had to play him as a family man'. Pulitzer Prize winning screenwriter David Mamet had

AL CAPONE.
He ruled Chicago
with absolute power.
No one could touch him.
No one could stop him.

Until Eliot Ness
and a small
force of men
swore they'd bring
him down.

THE **UNTOUCHABLES** 15

PARAMOUNT PICTURES PRESENTS AN ART LINSON PRODUCTION A BRIAN DE PALMA FILM
THE UNTOUCHABLES KEVIN COSTNER CHARLES MARTIN SMITH ANDY GARCIA
ROBERT DE NIRO as AL CAPONE and SEAN CONNERY as MALONE
Music by ENNIO MORRICONE Visual Consultant PATRIZIA VON BRANDENSTEIN Edited by JERRY GREENBERG Art Director WILLIAM A. ELLIOTT Director of Photography STEPHEN H. BURUM, A.S.C.
Written by DAVID MAMET Produced by ART LINSON Directed by BRIAN DE PALMA PANAVISION® DISTRIBUTED BY UNITED INTERNATIONAL PICTURES READ THE GRAFTON PAPERBACK DOLBY STEREO A PARAMOUNT PICTURE
ORIGINAL ALBUM AVAILABLE ON A&M RECORDS, CASSETTES AND COMPACT DISCS

The poster for *The Untouchables* (1987), Brian De Palma's successful movie version of the early 1960s TV series. 'Kevin wasn't famous. So what we did was surround him with people who were,' said the producer, Art Linson.

decided to soften the hard edge of the tough G-Man by giving Ness a wife and young child to worry over. Costner, by now the father of two daughters himself (Annie and Lily, who were three and one at the time) grinned and said: 'Nobody could tell me how to do that, but myself.'

The Untouchables is the story of how, in 1930, Special Agent for the U.S. Treasury Eliot Ness (Costner) sets out to clean up the streets of Chicago, and put out of business the hoodlum behind most of the crime – 'Scarface' Al Capone (Robert De Niro). Aware that the police force is riddled with corruption, he enlists the help of three men he can trust: a bespectacled accountant Oscar Wallace (Charles Martin Smith), a hot-headed Italian rookie cop George Stone (Andy Garcia) and tough, street-wise veteran Jim Malone (Sean Connery). Because they are oblivious to bribes and seemingly invincible, they become known, and feared, as 'The Untouchables'.

Waging his one-man war against Capone's empire almost like a publicity agent, Ness tips of the press before making a bust to guarantee getting the maximum publicity and to put the wind up the gang boss. 'I started making newspaper clippings and had the prop guy put them on a board to show my progress as Ness – "Ness Busts Out", "War Of Words Begins, Ness and Capone", "Ness Will Never Make It",' Costner recalled. But the problem was that Capone was never directly linked to the crimes. After a series of cat and mouse escapades with the mafia boss, Ness stumbles upon the loophole in the law-breaking that will prove to be Capone's downfall, and eventually send him to prison for 11 years: tax evasion.

Critics and filmgoers alike approved of *The Untouchables*. The realism and spectacular shoot-outs proved popular, and it was a great success at the box office – in America alone it grossed $74 million, making it the third biggest film of 1987 after *Platoon* and *Beverly Hills Cop II*. Fred Wehner in the British tabloid the *Daily Star* reckoned 'the key to this film's success is – you can't beat a good old story' and, acknowledging Costner's deviation from Robert Stack's 'unsmiling axe-wielding heavy who bulldozed his way into liquor warehouses and machine-gunned the Mafia hoodlums' noted that 'instead of a resolute man of steel, Eliot Ness is now a caring family guy who shows revulsion after killing'. Lester Middlehurst in the British tabloid *Today* agreed that 'Costner plays Ness in a way that is light years from Stack's TV role. Costner's Ness is handsome and uptight – Stack's was rough, tough and mean'.

Comparisons were inevitably drawn up between Costner's softly-softly approach and Stack's hard-hitting tough guy, with Costner perversely criticised for being too wimpish. Robert Stack, who won an Emmy for playing Ness, said: 'I played him tough and cold and methodical.' While Costner disagreed whole-heartedly: 'Ness was no Rambo,' he com-

mented at the time. 'I could have given him charm, I suppose. But instead I tried to make him a sensitive guy with a strong sense of duty and a revulsion for violence. He's really a desk man who's thrown in at the deep end. He's a rookie who learns the hard facts of life and death in Chicago as he goes along, and it toughens him up.' As Brian De Palma said, Eliot Ness was 'a white knight in a cesspool'.

Costner praised De Palma's concept: 'I think Brian should get an Oscar for that movie; it's a classic, it's a movie of genius. To take something that well known and change it so that you you don't think about history or the Robert Stack character; to recreate it so freshly, that was sheer brilliance.'

Costner continued: 'I hate it when people say that Eliot Ness is a wimp. I got a lot of

Sean Connery with Kevin Costner in *The Untouchables*. Costner admitted being in awe of the Scottish actor whom he admired greatly.

The Untouchables: (left to right) Charles Martin Smith, Kevin Costner, Sean Connery and Andy Garcia. Set in 1930, the film shows how, with the help of his three trusted operatives, Eliot Ness (Costner) finally nailed the arch mobster, Al Capone, memorably played by Robert De Niro, for tax evasion.

criticism for playing him that way, but I'll never play another character that kills more people. My only problem was justifying the bad language.'

Al Wolff, the original 'Untouchable' who had coached Costner, commented: 'Robert Stack was nowhere as good as Kevin Costner in acting like Ness. He was rough from the start. When the movie people took me out of the closet to show Costner how to act like Ness, I told him how to walk. Ness walked slowly. And I showed Costner how to use the gun. I said, "When you take a gun out, be ready to use it, because it's your life or their life." Parts of this was pretty real, but there was also a lot of Hollywood that they had to put in. But I enjoyed the movie. Costner did a good job. I was a good teacher.'

If Costner's character was deemed to be too wimpish, the same certainly did not apply to the star. Brian De Palma recalled how he had tried to talk Costner out of doing one particularly dangerous stunt on a tenement rooftop. 'It was a windy day in Chicago and this was 120 feet off the ground on top of a 12-storey building. We were all up there, and we got vertigo. Not Kevin. He had to walk about six inches from the edge. He's incredibly agile, which is very rare for a movie star. He moves like a dancer.'

'We determined before that I was going to take them - onstage and offstage - under my wing,' said Sean Connery, who won an Oscar for his portrayal of the street-wise veteran cop in *The Untouchables*.

Initially, the part of Ness had been dangled before Harrison Ford, Mel Gibson and William Hurt, but they were unavailable. But taking the gamble on a relative newcomer like Costner had worked out to be a wise move in the end. A new face in a well-loved role did not produce the kind of prejudice a star famous for other things might have done. 'Kevin is one of those actors who can make all the old clichés seem real again,' said director, Brian De Palma. The producer Art Linson said: 'There was no doubt in my mind that Kevin was the best for it. I wanted him as soon as I saw *Silverado*. He looked like a great Midwestern movie star to me – a very classic leading man with a Gary Cooper feel to him. I thought Eliot Ness had to be a true-blue American. Even if Mel Gibson had fixed his accent, there'd be something missing. Paramount was nervous: Kevin wasn't famous. So what we did was surround him with people who were.'

But Costner had become famous, and he wasn't so sure that he liked it. 'I have the same problem with stardom that I have with royalty,' he stressed. 'They're judged not by the quality of their work but by their birthright. I didn't set out to be a star. If you do, you engage in manipulation. You do stuff to be liked. I didn't want to be endorsed; I wanted to be listened to. I have ideas about things.'

Neither, regardless of plans by the publicity machine to the contrary, was

Costner prepared to accept the label movie star. 'If you want to see a movie star, talk to Sean Connery or Robert de Niro or Gene Hackman. I'm not a movie star, I'm an actor,' he argued. 'I don't think of myself as classically handsome. I've been told that the camera is good to me, but sometimes when people meet me, they're baffled.'

He shrugged off the suggestion that his new-found fame and wealth had changed his perspective on life, claiming that he still lived

a humble existence. 'Apart from being in movies, my life is quite ordinary. My lawn-mower wouldn't start this morning, for instance. I can't fix my car when it breaks down. I play characters who can. I don't understand certain financial things, though I'm really good with the bottom line.'

However, after *Silverado* and *The Untouchables*, people were beginning to recognize Costner in the street, and well-meaning fans started accosting him in bars and supermar-

kets. The down-side of fame was intruding. Yet there was something disingenuous about Costner's pained protestations about the loss of privacy success brought him, when he pushed himself onwards so assiduously, even ruthlessly. He has even admitted this, obliquely: 'I've always found it strange when people have great success, that seems to be the point when they often become a monster, because it strikes me that the time when you need to be a monster is when you're fighting your way up the ladder. You have to be a real gorilla then.'

During 1987, Costner also filmed *The Mission*, a segment of Steven Spielberg's TV anthology *Amazing Stories*. Like *The Twilight Zone* television series, the episodes involved mystery, suspense and the supernatural; *The Mission* was linked together with two other selections from the series – *Mummy Daddy* and *Go To The Head Of The Class* – to make a feature length movie. In Costner's segment, a World War II American air crew are flying a B-17 bomber on their 23rd mission over Occupied Europe. Led by Captain Spark (Costner), all is going according to plan until the plane is hit in a skirmish with a German fighter on the homeward leg of the flight. With one of the gunners, Jonathan (Casey Siemaszko), trapped in the bomber's floor turret and Spark unable to lower the wheels, the crew fear that he will be killed when Spark is forced to make an emergency 'belly landing' at their English airbase. They try to rescue their comrade, but to no avail. At the last minute, Jonathan – a budding cartoonist – draws a cartoon of the plane with the wheels down, and miraculously a set of magical wheels appear to bring it in safely. When Jonathan is freed from the tangled fuselage and dragged to safety, the wheels disappear.

Although far-fetched, it was typical of the type of escapist fantasy adventure of the fifties which Spielberg tried to revive. It was an unwise idea in retrospect, as the nostalgic series never caught on with the more sophisticated eighties audience who found it dated in concept, slightly banal and not all that different from the original *Twilight Zone* which was still being shown on some television channels.

In taking his next role, Costner disproved

Costner (right) as a World War II bomber captain in *The Mission*, one of three segments in Steven Spielberg's TV series *Amazing Stories* (1987) that were put together to be released as a movie.

Steven Spielberg (left) directing Costner and Casey Siemaszko in *The Mission*. It was Spielberg who recommended Costner for the role of Eliot Ness in *The Untouchables*.

the long-held Hollywood maxim that baseball movies are never hits. The decision to make *Bull Durham* (1988) came from his passion for the subject matter; it was a sport Costner had loved since childhood. The chance to play on the same pitch as the professional players drafted in to give some authenticity to the scenes, went some way towards fulfilling his earlier ambition of becoming a professional baseball player. 'If you're going to enter into anybody else's world, you should do as much as possible to honour it,' said the actor. 'That's problematic

By the time he made *Bull Durham* (1988) Kevin Costner was recognised as a major star, commanding nearly a million dollars a movie, but his off-set appearance was casual, a deliberate down-dressing typified by the clashing of smart trousers with scruffy sports shoes.

in certain films; in a sports film in particular, you can tell when a guy's not really an athlete.'

Costner was nervous and excited when he stepped on to the set on the first day, kitted out in his brand new baseball uniform. But he was slightly taken aback when he overheard the tough pros whisper: 'Here comes the fag from Hollywood.' Unwavering in the face of much nudging and winking, Costner scored points against the players by hitting a succession of home runs. 'I never acknowledged in college that I was a really good athlete,' he said. 'Had I chosen baseball over acting, I could have been a player. Everybody I went to high school with is gonna say "bull". But if I'd told the people I was gonna be an actor, they'd say "bull", too.'

This hard-edged side to Costner's personality, seldom seen so openly in public before, was much in keeping with that of his hard-headed character in *Bull Durham*, Crash Davis. Costner has compared this confrontation with the professional players to a similar scene in the film. He said: 'In the movie a

Costner with Susan Sarandon, his co-star in *Bull Durham*. It was Costner's idea to paint Susan Sarandon's toenails in bed in some of the sexiest scenes to be shown on screen.

boy urges, "Get a hit!" Most guys would rub the kid's head and say "I'll try". I snarl "Shut up".'

Costner added: 'I'd like there to be a little bit of Crash Davis in me – he had honour. He's not too good, not too bad, and if you can tap into his loyalty, I think Crash would be a very good friend. It's important to remember that Crash's saving grace is that he can laugh at the game he loves, and at

Kevin Costner checks the shot on location in *Bull Durham*. He had shown a keen interest in the technical side of film-making from the time of his first job as a stage manager at Raleigh Films, and few people were surprised when he became a director himself.

himself. And I even bought the car from the film.'

Crash Davis is a fading baseball player in a pretty bad team – the Class A Durham Bulls of the Carolina League – who is about to retire. He is asked by his coach to stay on another season to train their newest player, Ebby Calvin 'Nuke' LaLoosh (Tim Robbins). But Davis isn't the only veteran intent on coaching LaLoosh. Every season, college English teacher Annie Savoy (Susan Sarandon) picks one of the hottest new players to be her student in the art of love making. Spoilt for choice, she's unable to choose between LaLoosh and the ageing Davis, and tries to have both. Savoy feels oddly attracted to the ageing Davis, but fearing commitment plumps for the younger player. And anyhow, Davis tells Annie Savoy, he's not prepared to compete for her affections with a mere boy.

Soon Savoy brings confidence and worldly knowledge to the innocent LaLoosh, and it's not long before he's making a name for himself and getting transferred to a Major League team. LaLoosh's triumphant departure makes way for Davis to take up with Savoy, and they soldier on together in the face of Davis' growing frustration at becoming a has-been baseball player. Finally, Davis too decides to leave to play out his last season for another club so that he can break the record for the most league home runs in a career. After accomplishing his goal, Davis returns again to Savoy with plans to become a manager but more importantly to take life as it comes and hopefully make a go of things with her.

A highly-charged, sexy film with a typically Deep South downbeat humour, *Bull*

Coach 'Crash' Davis (Costner) becomes bitter towards his baseball prodigy 'Nuke' LaLoosh (Tim Robbins) when they both compete for the love of the same woman.

Durham was typified by the scene where Davis tells the philosophical Savoy: 'I don't believe in quantum physics when it comes to matters of the heart.' To which Savoy retorts: 'Well, what *do* you believe in then?'

Davis answers in his own inimitable way: 'Well, I believe in the soul, the cock, the pussy, the small of a woman's back, the hanging curveball, high fibre, good Scotch, that the novels of Susan Sontag are self-indulgent, overrated crap. I believe Lee Harvey Oswald acted alone. I believe there

ought to be a constitutional amendment outlawing astroturf and the designated hitter. I believe in the sweet pot, soft-core pornography, opening your presents Christmas morning rather than Christmas Eve, and I believe in long, slow, deep, soft, wet kisses that last three days. Good night.'

Critics liked Costner's honest portrayal of the down-on-his-luck Davis. 'Kevin Costner comes through with his first wide-awake, star performance,' wrote Pauline Kael in *The New Yorker*. 'He keeps you on his side from his very first scene...Costner lets you see that Crash is lonely, but he underplays loneliness; it's just a tone blended in with his other tones. He picks a fight with an umpire and goads the guy until he gets thrown off the field. (It's Costner's best scene: he's as berserkly ironic as Jack Nicholson is at some of his peaks.)' In *Time*, Richard Corliss wrote: 'Costner's surly sexiness finally pays off here; abrading against Sarandon's earth-mam geniality and Robbins' rude egocentricity, Costner strikes sparks.' And *Variety*'s verdict: 'Costner is a natural as the dyed-in-the-wool ballplayer. Overall, *Bull Durham* is a heck of a lot more involving than the average baseball game and wins out of sheer watchability and for its no-losers ending.'

If filmgoers thought sex in the limo with Sean Young in *No Way Out* was hot, it was nothing compared to the steamy table-top situations Costner found himself in with Susan Sarandon in *Bull Durham*. 'These are much sexier scenes,' he grinned. 'It's a 24-hour collision between a man and a woman. It's great.'

Although it was Costner who had thought up the idea of painting Susan Sarandon's toenails in bed (which he called 'a really cool thing'), he confessed to the American magazine *People Weekly*: 'I've not been comfortable with love scenes. You think about them the night before. You don't want to to be embarrassed. It's very difficult to get me to take off my shirt. I don't know why. I just feel awkward doing it. I've done it, but I just don't do it at the drop of a hat. I mean, I'm not a prude. You've seen my movies. I always depend on the script.' When the writer from *People Weekly* persisted, asking Costner what bothered him most about making love onscreen, the star laughed out loud and said: 'Now everybody knows how I kiss.'

Regardless of how difficult he finds love scenes, (he has claimed to feel more comfortable with a horse than a woman), Costner insisted that actresses always have it much harder. 'The actress is at a great disadvantage, because typically we show the actress more than we show the man, so there is this exploitative element, and if you like someone, you feel protective of her,' he said, adding that he had felt sorry for Sarandon and Young. 'I felt protective of Susan and Sean, because they're in a vulnerable position, so I didn't want to get lost in the acting so that something gets revealed that maybe they wouldn't want to be revealed.'

Susan Sarandon appreciated the concern that he had shown for her and felt that 'making *Bull Durham* with Kevin Costner was the best working experience I ever had. Kevin worries about all the right things. That's why he'll be a very good director.'

Costner has found it difficult to deal with his image as a 'sex symbol' and has been reluctant to discuss it. He told one British journalist: 'You hate asking me what it's like being a sex symbol and I hate telling you.' On the rare occasion when he has elaborated on the subject, he said: 'I always figured I was special, the way everybody is special. But I never thought I was sexy and I don't believe it now.'

Costner was reluctant to flaunt his body. He told *Rolling Stone* magazine that he never 'worked out' to keep in shape, nor attempted to develop his physical appearance: 'I'm not the kind of guy who hangs out at a gym. You don't find me lifting weights. I don't have

Costner as fading baseball star 'Crash' Davis in *Bull Durham*. An accomplished player himself, Costner was thrilled to have the opportunity to play with genuine professionals in the ballgame scenes.

those kinds of looks. I know now why women get intimidated looking at *Playboy*, saying, "This is what a woman is supposed to look like," because eighty-five percent of us walking around don't have what you would call extreme definition.'

After *Bull Durham*, Costner defied the movie pundits once again, ploughing straight into another baseball movie, *Field Of Dreams*. His role as a farmer with a vision brought him his first Academy Award nomination and helped him cross from stardom to super-stardom. 'I've been very lucky with stuff,' he said. 'But a lot of movies I end up doing no one really wants to make – I think people were laughing. Nobody wanted to make *No Way Out*, nobody wanted to make *Bull Durham*, and for the longest time nobody wanted to make *Field Of Dreams*.'

Costner as Ray Kinsella in *Field Of Dreams* (1989), tries to enlist the help of reluctant sixties activist and writer Terence Mann (James Earl Jones).

Costner continued: 'Most people I trusted thought I was nuts to make *Dreams*...When I first read *Field Of Dreams*, I thought it could be my generation's *It's A Wonderful Life*. It's the kind of movie that reminds me of why I like movies. You don't know how the story's going to end. It involves great characters, and it's ultimately poignant. Those are require-ments for me, really, for movies.'

Costner with Amy Madigan as his wife in *Field of Dreams*, the movie that earned him his first Oscar nomination.

Field Of Dreams (originally titled *Shoeless Joe*) is the story of Ray Kinsella, a poor farmer from Iowa, who dreams of creating a baseball park on his land even though the loss of crops will ruin him financially. At the beginning of the film Kinsella is seen walking through his cornfield when he suddenly hears a voice whisper: 'If you build it, he will come.' The 'he' is the legendary, though long-dead, baseball player Shoeless Joe Jackson, whom Kinsella comes to believe will return to play if he builds the park. Supported by his strong-willed wife Annie (Amy Madigan), Kinsella's dream becomes an obsession and he levels the land to the horror of the local community and in particular Annie's real-estate investor brother Mark (Timothy Busfield) who thinks he has gone crazy. Shoeless Joe does indeed come, bringing with him a ghostly all-star team. They appear every evening to play for Kinsella and family, though are invisible to everyone else.

However, the quest isn't over yet – with the threat of bankruptcy hanging over him, Kinsella goes in search of a sixties activist and writer Terence Mann (James Earl Jones), who in turn leads him to another former baseball player turned doctor, Archibald 'Moonlight' Graham (Burt Lancaster). It turns out that the Doctor too had died years earlier and Kinsella isn't sure of the significance...until travelling back to Iowa he picks up a young baseball-playing hitchhiker called Archie Graham (Frank Whaley), and the pieces begin to fall into place. More miraculous events occur, culminating in Kinsella's daughter Karin (Gaby Hoffman) being brought back to life after an accident; Kinsella healing his own big regret in life with his dead father who also comes back as a young ball player; and farm and field being saved.

The message was a simple one: it's never too late for second chances, to achieve lost opportunities, to say what you really feel, to do what you really want to do in life. A gentle, heart-warming story full of old-fashioned idealism, *Field Of Dreams* struck a chord with audiences and swiftly became one of 1989's biggest movies, grossing over $60 million in the US alone. The film's producer Lawrence Gordon said that even 'Arnold Schwarzenegger called us to tell us he couldn't stop crying.'

Praise from critics was unanimous. In America Gene Shalit on the NBC TV 'Today Show' hailed the film as 'a masterwork of wonderment.' Pat Collins for WWOR-TV deemed it to be 'The most original and appealing movie this year.' David Ansen in *Newsweek* described it as 'A magical and moving ride.' In Britain, Barry Norman said on BBC Television's 'Film 89' that he found it 'charming and magical...warm and moving', while Paul Gambaccini on TV-am voted it 'My favourite film of the year – 10 out of 10'.

'This is a different me,' Costner said shortly after the film's triumphant release. 'The fans are used to me being a guy with a lot of confidence, but this guy in *Field Of Dreams* is a bit of a bumbler. He is risking everything for his dream. Emotionally I believed it. But it scares [movie] people when there's no sex and no violence and no action for an audience as it waits for the ace card to be played. But that ace card can be so magical, it's just like a great love courtship. It can be worth the wait.'

All the previously 'essential' ingredients – violence, action, sex – were in plentiful

Burt Lancaster had a memorable cameo role as Archibald Graham, the baseball player turned doctor, in *Field Of Dreams*, seen here with Costner as Ray Kinsella and Gaby Hoffman as little Karin Kinsella.

supply in Costner's next picture. But in complete contrast to *Field Of Dreams*, which went totally against Hollywood tradition and became an enormous box-office hit, *Revenge* proved so unpopular with audiences that it failed to recover its costs when it was released in 1990.

Filmed on location in Mexico, *Revenge* was a torrid story of driven passion and sensuality which saw Costner stepping out of character to play an ex-US Navy pilot caught up in a deadly triangular relationship with a mafioso boss and wife. Costner knew he was taking a gamble by playing a 'bad' guy who steals another man's wife. '*Revenge* is a movie that's right on the edge,' he said at the time. 'Will people be really satisfied? I don't know because this movie ends in tragedy. It's not on an "up" ending. Maybe you won't even like me as a character.' He went on to explain that although this character was a drastic change for him, it was one he could live with: '*Revenge* is shocking, vulgar, a bit of a fall from grace. But I have no problem playing a man who isn't likeable, so long as I understand him. *Revenge* is strong medicine; you won't come out feeling good.'

Revenge follows the fortunes of retiring Vietnam veteran Cochran (Costner) when he

In 1989, Costner returned to the site of his honeymoon, Puerto Vallarta in Mexico, to shoot the erotic thriller *Revenge*.

decides to opt for a quieter life after twelve years military service flying jets. With nothing to do, he accepts an invitation from an old friend Tibey Mendes (Anthony Quinn) to stay at his palatial estate in Puerto Vallarta. He finds Tibey's beautiful new wife Miryea (Madeleine Stowe) irresistible. She is much younger than the wealthy and ruthless gangster, and is restless and unhappy tied to him. Inevitably Miryea and Cochran run off together. When Tibey discovers that they have become lovers, his vengeance is swift and brutal.

Beaten up and left in the desert to die, Cochran vows to settle the score with Tibey in the only way he will understand, but first he must seek out the missing Miryea, dumped by Tibey and his henchmen in a

brothel to be drugged and abused as her punishment.

A powerful and erotic adaptation of Jim Harrison's novella, *Revenge* was directed by Tony Scott against a shimmering backdrop of dusty deserts and golden suns. Originally the book was picked up by the late John Huston (who contributed to the script, but remains uncredited), but the idea lay dormant for a long time until Costner sought approval from Columbia to develop it himself, hence his executive producer credit. The final script was credited to Jim Harrison and Jeffrey Fiskin, but not before Costner had demanded several revisions and drafted in his friend Michael Blake to make additional re-writes. Costner said: 'While I was shooting *Field Of Dreams*, I called up and said, "This is the most awful script I've ever been connected to. It's equally as good a story as I've ever been part of." In 21 days, working between shots and on the way home in the car, we did a new script.'

Tony Scott did not mind Costner's interference: 'Directors always resent when an actor wants to make changes – especially a few weeks before shooting. But when Kevin pushed for lean and mean changes, he was right.' Costner said: 'Movies always threaten to go somewhere else, not because they are fragmented, that's the way they are shot. So you just become another eye looking out for the movie.'

While Kevin Costner was shooting *Revenge*, he was simultaneously trying to get his *Dances With Wolves* project off the ground. It is possible that the growing obsession with his Wild West dream distracted him from his work on *Revenge*. When the film opened to hostile reviews and poor cinema attendances,

Costner went onto the defensive. 'Right now, I don't know how this one will do,' he said. 'The movie is struggling to see what it can be. It hasn't completely sorted itself out so – it's not that I don't want to comment on it, it's just that I don't want to comment right now. I don't feel one way or the other about it yet.'

It can have been little solace for him that *Screen International* observed: 'It's easy to see why *Revenge* got made: on paper it must have sounded a great idea – a steamy love triangle, Mexican locations, and Kevin Costner getting a chance to show a mean side. Unfortunately though, *Revenge* just proves that a great movie takes more than pasting together a few good ideas.' *Newsweek* deemed it as 'lurid and basic as the title', while *New York* magazine stated: '*Revenge* may be sexy and violent, but it's also lethally boring.' The British film magazine *Empire* was the most forthright: 'A fairly nasty piece of work all round, and a critical and box-office turkey that would suggest that Costner being mean and nasty is not the Costner many folk wish to pay to see.'

Even after all the production problems, the slating from critics, and the rejection by audiences, Costner defended the film. 'I had to use my considerable weight at the box office to get the movie made,' he said. 'To me, it's like picking a football team. The story makes sense and it was obvious that I should play quarterback or end. I mean, Cochran is a role that I should have played.'

Costner as the Vietnam veteran Cochran with Madeleine Stowe as the hoodlum's wife he seduces in *Revenge*. The gamble to step out of character and pay a bad guy backfired when the movie flopped badly at the box-office.

Chapter Four

Dances With Wolves

WHEN Michael Cimino's grandiose 3½ hour epic *Heaven's Gate* failed disastrously in 1980, it confirmed what film-makers had feared for some time – that the end of the Western as a safe-bet formula was imminent. The modern day king of cowboys Clint Eastwood had signalled the change in audience tastes as early as 1976. While making *The Outlaw Josey Wales* that year, he confessed: 'Some executives from some studio came out and said, "Westerns aren't doing anything" and the general Hollywood studio wisdom was to avoid completely the previously cast-iron genre. Even big names like Newman,

As the culmination of years of single-minded effort to get *Dances With Wolves* on to the screen, Costner was rewarded with seven Oscars, including those for best film and best director.

Nicholson, Brando and, unthinkably, Wayne weren't drawing audiences to the box-office.

Western themes were being surpassed by the escapism of space films, the seat-clenching special effect shockers in horror movies and the fast-action cop movies that seemed to explode onto the screen. The more sophisticated audiences of the eighties, who had become accustomed to such stupefying characters as Indiana Jones and Freddy Krueger, had simply found cowboy movies old hat.

In this climate, *Dances With Wolves* was the biggest gamble of Costner's career. Originally Hollywood film-makers rejected the idea of the story. It was bad enough that it was a Western, but the fact that the film questioned the ethics of how the white man had almost annihilated the native Americans, that Costner intended to show things from the

Indians' point of view – that was just too much. As a first-time director, co-producer and star Costner performed miracles in even getting a production deal going. But he defied the movie experts who warned him that Westerns were passé, that at three hours the film was too long, and audiences would not like subtitles. Costner revealed how one studio head had told him: 'Buy a gun and shoot yourself in the head – it will be a quicker and cheaper way to commit suicide.' In scathing attacks on Costner's pretensions as an actor-director, and with reference to Cimino's self-indulgent *Heaven's Gate*, critics described *Dances With Wolves* as 'Kevin's Gate'. When *Dances* ran over its $16 million budget, they called it 'Costner's last stand'. One critic, Pauline Kael in *The New Yorker,* even went as far as saying: 'Costner has feathers in his hair and feathers in his head.'

Costner later admitted: 'I knew *Wolves* was very ambitious. I didn't know whether I could direct but I knew that I would have to die trying. The idea that I might not be able to do this kept me up at night. I told studio heads this is not standard movie fare but if I can make it become what I have in my mind people will want to go to the theatre.'

Dances With Wolves is a sweeping Wild West adventure, set in 1863. As the Sioux nation lives its last years on the unspoilt lands, a civil war rages in the eastern part of the country. A hero of that war, Lt. John J. Dunbar (Costner), chooses reassignment to the West as a reward for his act of bravery, following a lifelong dream to see the frontier before it disappears. On his arrival on the Dakota prairie Dunbar discovers that he is the sole inhabitant of the abandoned Fort Sedgewick, but undeterred assumes his post.

Seemingly all alone in this vast and beautiful wilderness, with only a curious wolf and his horse for company, Dunbar soon comes in to contact with the noble Sioux, including the tribal chief Ten Bears (Floyd Red Crow Westerman), Kicking Bird (Graham Greene), and the proud young brave Wind In His Hair (Rodney Grant). Soldier and Sioux slowly overcome their distrust for one another and develop mutual respect and admiration. Dunbar is eventually accepted into the tribe and renamed Dances With Wolves. In due course, he strikes up a relationship with the grieving widow Stands With A Fist (Mary McDonnell), a white woman raised by the Sioux as one of their own after her family was killed by the warring Pawnee tribe.

The film traces the growth of Dunbar's friendship with the Sioux, follows his romance with Stands With a Fist, the conflicting loyalties he feels between his duty as a soldier and the discovery of his true place on earth. As a man in search of himself, he is ultimately faced with the hardest decision of his life by the arrival of the U.S. army.

Dances With Wolves is the story of one man's dream and the labour of love of three friends: a writer, a producer and a director. The almost story book way the film came about in its conception showed how it was always going to be something special. Writer Michael Blake and producer Jim Wilson had become close friends with Kevin Costner in the years that followed the filming of *Stacy's Knights* in 1981. But whereas Costner had gone on to international stardom, Blake and Wilson were not so fortunate. Wilson had produced a video feature, *Laughing Horse,* in 1984 and directed *The Movie Maker* in 1986, but apart from these two ventures, he had failed to realise his vocation as a top film-maker. Blake, on the other hand, had fared even worse. As a struggling screenwriter he was forced to take a variety of menial jobs in pill factories, Christmas tree lots and dish-washing rooms to keep him going. To his credit, Blake kept on writing. 'I wrote the entire book in my car,' he has claimed. 'I couldn't pay my rent. It was either get a job and have an apartment or write the book and be on the street – so I chose the latter. I was like a tramp.'

Wilson had followed the progress of Blake's novel with a keen interest. Often the homeless writer would stay over at Wilson's house and read chapters of the unpublished manuscript to him and his wife. Wilson later recalled: 'I thought immediately that the character of Lieutenant Dunbar would be ideal for Kevin, and once he had read the manuscript, he too agreed.'

At that time, 1988, Blake was working as a dishwasher in a Chinese restaurant. He had become disillusioned with his lack of success in trying to find a publisher, and in a moment of desperation dropped the manuscript off at Costner's home 'to see what he thought'. With Costner's growing professional stature and far-reaching contacts, Blake felt that if anyone could help him, then surely Costner could. But as Costner has admitted, with *Bull Durham* almost completed and him about start filming *Field Of Dreams*, he was simply too busy for his friend's book: 'I didn't read it for two months after it was done. It was a doorstop for me.'

Thanks to Blake's persistence and a partic-ularly harsh winter Costner finally got round to looking at the manuscript. As he remem-bered it: 'It was the time we sent Michael a boxful of sleeping bags and stuff, and he asked me if I'd had the chance yet to read his book. That's when I just said, "That's it!". And I read it and it was the clearest idea for a movie that I'd ever read.' Costner loved *Dances With Wolves* so much, he virtually financed Blake while he wrote the screenplay. Though Blake later confessed that Costner had caused him much grief when the actor forced him to re-write the script six times until he was satisfied. 'Kevin's visions don't always line up exactly with mine,' Blake said on the set of *Dances With Wolves*. 'Sometimes I walk out and I look at the way something is being done and I think "I would do it that way". There have been some times when I thought Kevin would fall flat on his face, that he was totally wrong. But he proved himself right – so I don't bet against Kevin Costner.'

Before filming began, Costner made a pilgrimage to the site of Custer's last stand, The Battle Of The Little Big Horn, in Montana. He had hinted at his reasons for going there when he said: 'I've had two recurrent nightmares in my life. One was that I was on the *Titanic*, the other was that I was at Custer's Last Stand – I know that's strange, but it's true.' And he added proudly: 'I'm part Cherokee and part German. I read a book about General Custer and discovered his real German name was Kosta, which is very like Costner. I had to go to the Little Big Horn because I've always thought of myself as a pioneer in a previous life.'

Nevertheless, in deciding to co-produce, direct and star in an epic Western that he had helped conceive, Costner had undoubtedly taken a sizeable personal risk. While it was unlikely that his stature as a leading star would be affected if *Dances With Wolves* had

Kevin Costner with his long-time friend and business associate Jim Wilson at the Golden Globe awards. As producer of *Dances With Wolves* and a co-director of Costner's company Tig Productions, Jim Wilson has been closely involved in Costner's success.

failed, it would almost certainly have shaken his credibility in gaining finance for further projects for himself and his development company, Tig Productions, which he set up with Jim Wilson. Not surprisingly Costner was full of self-doubt about his abilities to carry the film through. 'My apprehensions going into it were that I wouldn't make it a great movie, and I needed for it to be a great movie.' Costner added that he had even considered other people directing the film: 'Every time I talked about the project there was a sense that they saw things in it they thought the movie didn't need, or couldn't absorb, and I thought to myself, "I'm not sure of that." And I began to question how they could be so sure that the movie didn't need to have this or that. I suddenly realised that maybe I should direct it, because otherwise I'd be forever frustrated if the simplicity I saw in this story was lost as a result of not taking enough time.'

From the very beginning Jim Wilson believed in his friend's instincts as a director: 'I believed in him implicitly, having seen him in workshops, working with actors, and on location. But I guess there was a question mark against him, not having directed before,' he conceded. 'How Kevin would handle his multiple roles was the biggest question prior to shooting. I knew he had incredible stamina – but the fact was that his

character is present in all but a few scenes, while at the same time he's directing, seeing to production details, and doing most of his own stunts. This all had to go on for 108 gruelling days of filming.'

Costner admitted that directing *Dances With Wolves* was the single most difficult thing he had ever done, and said that he had learned more things about himself doing it

very good with action scenes. When you punch a guy in the face, there's probably a great angle to it, an ideal place to put the camera. I don't know those angles, but I feel that I understand drama. So whenever I got into problems I pointed the camera at what I felt the truth was.'

Costner continued passionately: 'As a director, you have to remind somebody what it's like to breathe, what it's like to be out of air. You have to remind him that someone's being killed two feet away from him. You have to remind him that the horse he's trying to get on represents life and death.' He added: 'Someone told me, "Look, there's no doubt you're going to stay up all night thinking about where you're going to put the camera the first time, to look like you know what you're doing." But it's not where you set the camera down the first time that's the challenge. It's where do you put it the second time? And every time after that. It's how to sustain the imagination.'

Mary McDonnell, who played Costner's lover in the film, Stands With A Fist, described how Costner was excited by the actors' ideas, things he hadn't thought of, and how he was open to suggestions. 'In one romantic scene,' she explained, 'we were embracing, and there was something he wanted to communicate to me as a director, so during the actual take he whispered directions into my ear, and it was always like that; we'd get lost in who he was – the director or the actor.'

Perhaps the most awkward moment for Costner was having to direct his own nude scene, where his character Dunbar bathes by a river bank. 'I've been involved in scenes in bathtubs and bedrooms and on kitchen

than from any other experience in his life. 'I think I did a good job, but that would just be a personal assessment, because I'm quite sure there are people out there saying, "This guy doesn't know what he's doing."' His initial fear of failure behind him, Costner rose to the challenge of directing. 'I liked it a lot,' he said. 'Whenever I got into trouble, I went back to the drama of the story. See, I wasn't tables, but I never feel comfortable when I have to take my shirt off,' he said. 'The nude scene in *Dances With Wolves* was in the book and I think it was essential to show my character's vulnerability. I had to set up the shot, take off my clothes and walk out there, relying on other people to tell me if you could see too much.' He added: 'I found the biggest reeds I could hide behind.'

For Jim Wilson, as producer, one of the main tasks facing him in the first few weeks was to find the right location for shooting the movie. He explained: 'I needed America in the 1860s, complete with tribes of Native Americans, herds of buffalo and horses, endless prairie vistas with rivers and snow-capped mountains – all within driving distance of a city that could support our crew of 200-plus. Needless to say, we did a lot of flying, scouting locations in eight states as well as Canada and Mexico.'

Despite an extensive search of Oklahoma and Texas, areas where the Comanche Indians in Blake's novel existed, Wilson was finally forced to settle for South Dakota where the many buffalo needed for the crucial hunt scene were greater in numbers. Striving to maintain as much authenticity as possible, this choice of location was also the reason for the changing of the tribe to Sioux in the movie. By chance, Wilson had heard that a former lieutenant governor of the state, Roy Houck, kept the largest private herd of buffalo in the world – some 3,500 head – at his ranch outside the state capital of Pierre.

As luck would have it, South Dakota also had the added benefit of one of the largest Native American communities in the country, the Sioux. 'Casting the Native Americans was a challenge,' Wilson recalled.

'We hired actors from all over the U.S. and Canada, and many tribes other than the Sioux participated – though 250 Sioux from the South Dakota reservations worked as extras. One criterion was that we had to have people with an authentic period look, and a lot of urban Indians had cut their hair, or didn't have the right look. But our casting director, Elizabeth Leustig, did an incredible job finding people who not only looked the part but brought the characters to life.' From the onset the director had decreed that a fine attention to detail was to be paramount. Costner stated firmly: 'It seems to me that when you make a movie that deals with Native Americans, you should be using the best ones you can find that have the most presence and soul about them.'

During pre-production creative designers travelled throughout the West and South-west gathering historical information. Their intensive research took them to libraries, archives and museums for rare pictures, artefacts and documentation. Production designer Jeff Beecroft said: 'Kevin wanted to offer a reality that hasn't been seen on the screen before. He wanted to convey a West that was wild and untamed and larger than life, as seen through the eyes of Dunbar, who comes from the East.' Elsa Zamparelli, costume designer, insisted at the time: 'The costumes we made are very traditional and made exactly right – the same old beads that were used a hundred years ago, the same buckskin – and it's very labour-intensive.' She added: 'All the Indian actors are wearing their own eagle feathers, for a very good reason. We're not allowed to use them, because eagles are endangered. But it's legal for the Indians to have them, and in a lot of cases they've been passed down from older family members.'

Kevin Costner and Mary McDonnell learned to speak Lakota, one of several Sioux dialects, in the subtitled sequences as did most of the Indian actors who belonged to tribes other than the Sioux. The producers were fortunate in having the assistance of Doris Leader Charge, an instructor of Lakota language and culture at Sinte Gleska College on the Rosebud Reservation in Rapid City, South Dakota. She remembered when the film was first brought to her attention: 'Jim Wilson called me and asked if I'd like the chance to read the script. And I said I don't know about that because I've never ever seen one. And he said, "Well, do you think you could?" And I said I don't now – I'd have to see it first and he went and asked if Federal Express came out to the reservation? And I said yeah.'

Leader Charge also appears in *Dances With Wolves*, playing the role of Pretty Shield, the wife of chief Ten Bears. She added: 'I was scared about doing this movie at the beginning, but it's been a good experience. It portrays us as we really are. They've gotten it right this time.'

The Sioux were once a great tribe who roamed almost 50 million acres of American territory, land that has now become Nebraska, Wyoming, Montana and North and South Dakota. In the 100 years that have elapsed since the soldiers defeated the Sioux at the Battle of Wounded Knee, the tribe has dwindled to around 60,000 surviving members, most of whom live on the two million acre reservations in South Dakota. These areas to which the US government has restricted the Sioux are amongst the poorest in America. Poverty, crime and high unemployment are rife there. It was this injustice that inspired author Michael Blake to write *Dances With Wolves*. 'When I think what was lost in the trampling of the great horse culture and its people, I am made immeasurably sad,' he said. 'Here were a people living in rough perfection; at home with sky, earth, and plain; strong families living in societies that valued and cared for their members. Not only was most of this destroyed but what little remained was locked up in reservations in desolate territory, far from public sight.'

He continued: '*Dances With Wolves* was written in part because I wanted to present some of the record of history as I see it. It was my hope that showing what was lost, something might be regained – not the least of which could be new respect for the proud descendants of the people I wrote about, who are living yet on reserves where our ancestors confined them.'

Today, many of the younger members of the community are still full of bitterness and resentment. According to Rodney A. Grant, who played Wind In His Hair, wariness of the white man's Native American prejudice had been brought home to him when he returned to the area near the South Dakota reservation where he was brought up to make the movie. In an interview with *Today* he described how he had been kept under close surveillance by a local police officer upon entering a better neighbourhood of the small town of Walthill. Grant claimed that, 'Until they realised we were involved in the movie and were "celebrities" we were just potential muggers and rapists. Everywhere you went you got hostility and anger. The hate was still there.'

Grant went on to say that he was extremely sceptical when he first heard about *Dances With Wolves*. 'We thought it was just "Cowboys and Indians again",' he admitted. 'And we were very suspicious of Kevin. We had no reason to suspect his intentions were any different. But he *was* different. He went out of his way to be normal. He talked to us about his wife and kids and he asked us if we felt he was going the wrong way. We had nothing but respect for him. He wanted to be our friend. He expected friendship in return.'

Costner was accused of re-writing history to make a political point about the plight of the native Americans. 'Until *Dances With Wolves* Indians were monosyllabic savages on screen,' he has said. 'I think *Wolves* captured for the first time the essence of how Indians may really have been. It gave me great satisfaction that Indians loved my film and proclaimed me their friend.' Costner went on to explain how he hoped people would remember him as a man who had brought awareness of the atrocities into the open. 'It is a fact that we have committed genocide in this country and that we have chosen to ignore that fact. We like to point to South Africa or Hitler. We are aware of what other people have done, but we tend to ignore what we have done to the American Indian. We turn our back on it. But we destroyed a people and a culture to get what we wanted.'

In the 1970s a conscious attempt was made to demythologize native Americans and present their culture and creeds as authentically as possible. But seen through the eyes of the white man they were invariably constrained. *A Man Called Horse* saw Richard Harris strung up in the flesh-ripping Sioux Sun Dance ritual. *Little Big Man* had Dustin Hoffman as an adopted Indian who witnesses the harsh treatment of his tribe. And *Soldier Blue* saw Candice Bergen caught up in the carnage of the Sand Creek Indian massacre of 1864.

Costner was determined that his film should give as dignified a presentation of the Sioux as possible. 'I showed them thinking about their situation, which in the past films have tended not to do,' he said. 'During the shooting of *Dances*, some Indian actors turned up on the set one day without having learned their lines. I reminded them that this was a project about their people, that if it didn't turn out, they'd be embarrassed, not me. I warned them that if they were cavalier with my time, there had better be a good reason.'

Graham Greene, who plays the medicine man Kicking Bird, is a full-blooded Oneida, one of the Iroquois tribes, born on the Six Nations Reserve in Ontario, Canada. He gratefully acknowledged Costner's help in reclaiming some of his own Indian heritage: 'I was brought up without much sense of my Indian heritage, and now I'm slowly learning what my people were and the traditions behind them.' he said. Author Michael Blake added: 'Graham is a good example of how this movie was cast – the Indians are human beings first, not just types. You see it in his appearance at the fort, when he just walks around calmly and thoughtfully checking things out. He doesn't creep around like an aborigine.' Costner agreed: 'He doesn't come off right away as a strong Indian "type", so at first I saw just the professional actor rather than some sculptured guy that maybe I was looking for.'

In addition to the Native Americans,

Costner was responsible for overseeing 130 crew members, 500 extras, 3,500 buffalo, 300 horses, 42 old west wagons and several warehouses full of props. The buffalo hunt alone involved a helicopter, 10 pick-up trucks, 24 bareback Indian riders, 150 extras, 20 wranglers to handle the herd of buffalo, 25 recreated buffalo and seven cameras. Though it lasts only four minutes on screen, the hunt is one of the most complex animal scenes ever filmed; the eight gruelling days of shooting were as carefully planned and boldly executed as a military operation. The giant 1,600lb bovines were carefully monitored to avoid any harm or injury and several trained animals were brought in to handle some of the special effects. In addition, 25 artificial buffalo – built from foam and fibreglass, with fur coverings – were used to portray the fallen animals. One was fitted with complex pneumatics that simulated breathing and kicking, while another – which was set up on a dolly with collapsing legs – was used for a running fall shot. For all the impressive technology on display, some of the primitive techniques employed by the special-effects experts at Kurtzman, Nicotero & Berger EFX Group were more reminiscent of Hollywood in its heyday. As KNB's Greg Nicotero admitted to *People Weekly*: 'Sometimes we'd just set the camera on the ground and roll one of the fake buffalo in front of it and kick up a bunch of dust.'

One of the main problems with using the buffalo on such a grand scale was trying to contain them in the vast open space of the prairie. Even before they could begin the stampede it took wranglers six hours to round up the herd and get them charging. The fact that it took a mere five minutes for the herd to race past the seven camera crews – and another ten miles until they ground to a halt, gives a fair indication as to why the scene took so long to film. Costner was full of praise for the eighteen veteran Indian riders who galloped bareback amid the stampeding herd: 'The very first day the buffalo ran, there were three thousand of them coming at us, and nobody was sure what was going to happen. The Native American riders were wild and they were great rodeo riders, but no one had ridden among the buffalo for more than a hundred years. So no one knew what to expect, really, and suddenly here they came over the hill, and people's stomachs were in their throats...'

He added: 'All of a sudden one buffalo started to bolt in the wrong direction, and that's when I knew these guys [the riders] were committed. They were afraid, but they threw their horses in front of those buffalo and tried to salvage that run.'

Costner insisted on doing his own stunts during the hunt, riding alongside the Indians and firing his gun without reins. But he had a terrifying brush with death when another horse veered out of control and crashed into his mount, tossing him from the saddle. He hit the ground as thousands of thundering buffalo hooves pounded around him. As Costner remembered it, 'The great thing about that moment was that my stunt coordinator, Norman Howell, immediately bolted out and just said, "How are you?" I said, "I'm fine – give me your horse." And he looked at me and just made the decision to do it, no more questions. Right in the middle of that chaos he calmly rebridled the horse in a split second so I could get back into the hunt.' Jim Wilson, who was watching from overhead in the helicopter, described how Costner must have felt during the filming of the hunt: 'He doesn't say a whole lot when he's nervous, but he had to be scared. The buffalo would come charging down a hill, and all of a sudden the riders would kick their mounts into gear, and they'd be flying amongst them.' Costner's wife Cindy was also present on set. 'I was so nervous I really was making myself physically ill. I couldn't tell him what to do when he was directing *Dances*. At night I could chew on him a little bit, but he was gonna go out there the next day and do what he wanted to do.'

Costner enjoyed the security and support of having his family around him on location. Keen to become involved in her husband's work, Cindy Costner was given the responsibility of rounding up the 42 period wagons for the movie, a task she carried out admirably. She also helped out with serving food to the crew at mealtimes in the canteen tent. As a reward, she and the children were cast as extras in the brief flashback sequence where Stands With A Fist remembers her last day as a little girl called Christine, when the Pawnee attacked and slaughtered her family. 'I know people wonder why I gave those roles to my family,' Costner answered to charges of nepotism. 'Well, I just did it and I can't explain why. I never want to be a stranger to my kids, so I make them very much a part of my life.' But even his children – Annie, Lily and Joe, who were six, four and two at the time – did not escape the wrath of their perfectionist father. Costner has admitted that on one occasion he almost went too far while directing Annie. He described how she had been up on a roof and was supposed to look frightened, but that she had trouble

trying to look convincing enough. Costner went on, 'And so I pushed her a bit, and we still didn't get there, and I debated about whether to push her some more, but I thought I'd give her a five-minute break first.'

He continued: 'So I looked down at her, and she was looking at me, and I said, "You're doing great, honey." And her lip started to quiver, and she said, "I'm awful." And when she started to cry, that movie became so important to me – nothing mattered. It made me grow up a little bit.'

As well as trying to overcome the problem of the buffalo and the inexperience of his children in front of the camera, Costner had heard that wolves were among the most difficult animals to work with. But as Jim Wilson had so rightly pointed out to him, if they were going to have the name *Dances With Wolves*, and did not use real wolves, it would have been a travesty. Wilson has admitted that they did consider using half-breeds, malamutes or huskies. 'They may look like a wolf, but they don't walk like a wolf,' he explained. 'Wolves have a very distinctive way of walking on those long, thin legs, and the wolf lope is unmistakable.' Two Socks, the wolf in *Dances*, was played by a pair of timber wolves, Buck and Teddy, provided by veteran trainers Gale Phelps and Sled Reynolds. The reason

Costner was formally 'adopted' by the Rosebud Tribal Sioux Nation as a brother of Sinte Gleska College for outstanding representation of the Lakota Sioux Nation.
However, some critics accused him of re-writing history to highlight the plight of the Native Americans.

for having the two animals was that Buck was good at pondering, Teddy at pacing and trotting to a spot. As they were dangerous and unpredictable, filming was conducted on a closed set cleared of children and using the minimum of crew members. Costner's only protection during the nine days' shoot was a fine wire the wolves were trained not to cross. As Jim Wilson said in *People Weekly*: 'You don't just say, "Wolf, go bite Kevin's leg."'

Sceptics had warned Costner right from the beginning that he was crazy in his directorial debut to take on such a problematic period film involving the challenge of shooting in all four seasons. 'It's a dumb first movie... full of kids, animals, first-time actors speaking in a foreign language. A period piece on top of that,' he said on one occasion. People told him that with the limited amount of money he had at his disposal, it simply couldn't be done. At one point *Dances With Wolves* fell two weeks behind schedule and Costner began overspending his $16 million budget. When the loan companies who had backed the film sent insurance bondsmen to the set, Costner agreed to forfeit part of his $5 million salary to help ease the financial burden (he deferred $2.9 million to cover costs). In a scathing attack on the companies who had put up the money, Costner accused the businessmen of destroying the film industry. 'Most people don't know how much these companies hurt movies,' he said. 'I guess they're necessary for the business but I don't like dealing with them.'

Costner also revealed how he had offered to buy them out to stop them interfering; he had been livid at their suggestion that he cut some of the film's best scenes – namely the buffalo hunt and subtitled sequences – which they had deemed to be unimportant. He continued: 'I offered to buy out these cowards. I said "I'll pay your salary, just get the fuck out of my life." That shocked the shit out of them. They are necessary for people who do runaway things. But to people who are fiscally responsible, they're a giant pain in the ass. They endanger a project that's trying to run the line. They start telling you you can't do things. I ended up doing everything I wanted.' And he flatly refused when an airline company stepped in and offered to bail him out with a $4 million offer if he would edit the film down for in-flight screening. 'They wanted to cut it down to two hours. But I just couldn't bear the thought of people seeing an edited version. I decided not to take the money even though I desperately needed it at the time.'

After a three-year struggle to make the film, Costner's unflagging commitment to *Dances With Wolves* was acknowledged when it received three Golden Globe awards in 1991: Best Picture, Best Screenplay and, for Costner, Best Director. Clutching his awards at the ceremony, Costner was clearly delighted: 'One night doesn't make a career. But it feels as good as you might think it feels.' If Costner was a happy man then, he was astounded when *Dances* later received 12 Oscar nominations. It matched the 12 gained by *Reds* in 1981 – and was one short of the record 13 nominations for *Who's Afraid Of Virginia Woolf?* in 1966.

At the 63rd annual Academy Awards ceremony in 1991, watched by an estimated one billion television viewers in 80 different countries, *Dances With Wolves* won an incredible seven Academy Awards: Best Picture,

Best Director, Best Cinematography, Best Screenplay, Best Original Score, Best Sound, and Best Film Editing. When Costner stepped up on the stage with his friend and co-producer Jim Wilson to accept the Best Picture trophy from Barbra Streisand, he told the 6,000-strong celebrity audience at the Shrine Auditorium in Los Angeles: 'I will never forget what happened here tonight. *Dances With Wolves* won this year, and while it's not as important as the rest of the world situation, it will always be important to us.'

As the stars celebrated afterwards, Costner was non-committal about a possible sequel to *Dances With Wolves*. Although Michael Blake, jubilant about his Oscar-winning screenplay, had announced his plans to write a follow-up called *Holy Road*, Costner was understandably concerned about the far-reaching effects of having such a huge film to his name. 'I hope *Dances With Wolves* doesn't prove such a monster that I am unable to get out of its shadow,' he said.

Going by the accolades he also received from critics, Kevin Costner had a lot to live up to. 'He has made an extraordinarily fine film, but the finest thing in it is himself,' said Iain Johnstone in the *Sunday Times*. 'In his directorial debut, Kevin Costner brings a rare degree of grace and feeling to this elegiac tale,' declared *Variety*. 'Breathtakingly forged by first-time director Kevin Costner,' wrote Duane Byrge in *The Hollywood Reporter*. 'It's an engrossing tale, and Costner directs with the confidence of a Hollywood veteran,' enthused David Ansen in *Newsweek*. 'A marvellous story, a satisfying blend of urgent action and adventure with one man's voyage to discovery,' said the *Daily Mail*. 'A compassionate, romantic, occasionally exciting epic

that combines ideals, emotion and solid entertainment,' said *Screen International*.

In his introduction to the accompanying book *Dances With Wolves: The Illustrated Story Of The Epic Film*, which he wrote with Michael Blake and Jim Wilson, Kevin Costner laid bare some of his innermost feelings about the making of the movie. It is fitting that the final word on the film should be his:

'*Dances With Wolves* was in fact born out of a personal challenge, the seed of which came out of a conflict that could easily have torn the fabric of a long friendship. It will forever be to Michael Blake's credit that *Dances* was conceived and my great luck to be associated with it...that Michael would write about the American frontier was in many ways a complete surprise. That I loved it was not. Michael managed to forge all the elements most attractive to me – simplicity, dignity, humour, and poignancy. He created a story that embraced a culture that has traditionally been misrepresented, both historically and cinematically.

'That *Dances* was a movie was clear. Whether I should direct this movie was probably the biggest question. It became both a personal and a professional battle. The one thing I knew, however, was that if *Dances* in the smallest way was not as great as the movies that had shaped my love of them, I would always regret my decision...

'If I am blessed with good health, there is little doubt that I will make other movies, but if I could not, *Dances With Wolves* would complete the picture I have had of myself since I was a little boy. It will forever be my love letter to the past.'

Chapter Five

Prince of Hollywood

WHEN *Robin Hood: Prince of Thieves* opened in America in June 1991, the critics savaged it. Costner in particular was singled out for his 'dull, hapless' performance and 'bland surfer-speak' accent. 'Where's Errol Flynn when we need him?' cried one. 'We've been robbed!' scoffed another. Even the *New York Daily News*, a publication generally renowned for its generosity towards turkeys, couldn't resist a swipe at the film's scapegoat star: 'Costner plays a tortured, thoughtful Robin Hood, totally lacking in the joy of living we associate with the character.' Meanwhile *USA Today* simply sneered: 'He can swing a baseball bat

Although *Robin Hood: Prince of Thieves* proved to be one of the most successful films of the nineties, Kevin Costner had misgivings about the production at the start.

and dance with wolves, but Spartacus he'll never be.' The *Los Angeles Daily News* deemed it 'one long embarrassment', an opinion shared by the *New York Times,* which declared it 'a mess, a big, long joyless reconstruction of the legend'. In spite of this critical blasting the film was an instant success at the box office, recovering its $60 million costs within days. *Variety* couldn't ignore this, but was grudging. 'Kevin Costner's Robin Hood is a Robin of wood,' wrote its reviewer. 'No matter how much coin is raked in, total could have been a lot better had it been a good film.'

When the film reached the UK a month later, in the middle of July, the hail of arrows continued to bombard Costner, though more cautiously; whereas critics agreed tentatively with their American colleagues on certain aspects of the film's shortcomings, they wisely conceded it would 'no doubt' do big business due to its star's following, and the attention generated by much pre-release hype by Warner Brothers. Derek Malcolm, reviewing the film in *The Guardian,* was quick to point out the irony of the hostile reaction it suffered in the States. 'Ever since then it's been a hit,' he remarked. 'What do critics know about anything?'

It was enough to make John Powers in *Sight and Sound* proclaim, 'Every critic I know is depressed by its huge popularity: the movie serves up big budget film-making at its most slipshod, but the audience doesn't seem to care or even notice.' Ian Lyness began his review in *The Daily Express*: 'Forget the carping of US critics. Kevin Costner's Robin Hood is right on target as a roller-coaster ride of thrills and laughs...If you're looking for sheer entertainment, this hits the bullseye.' *The Daily Mail*'s Shaun Usher also liked the 'boys' own' adventure aspects: 'A super bout of escapism, fast, slick, and handsomely mounted.' And George Perry conceded in *The Sunday Times* that, despite its flaws, the film still managed to be 'highly enjoyable'.

But it was Alan Rickman's scene-stealing Sheriff of Nottingham that captivated critics most, with an over-the-top comic performance that leaned heavily on knock-about camp. Following an early test screening in America, at which the audience unanimously voted Rickman's sheriff as their favourite character, way ahead of Costner's Robin, the film's makers, Morgan Creek Productions, were said to have edited out some of Rickman's scenes in favour of more close-ups of Costner.

If the producers were worried that their superstar was being upstaged by the English Shakespearian actor, their actions to counter this failed. *The Hollywood Reporter* declared Alan Rickman 'a pure delight'. 'He is clearly having a ball,' wrote the reviewer, 'as he relentlessly mugs the camera.' Garth Pearce, one of the few journalists allowed on set, wrote in *The Sunday People:* 'The movie may have been doctored to beef up Costner's role – but the baddie still manages to upstage the hero. Mr Rickman steals so many scenes being funny ha-ha as well as funny peculiar that even the star's persona...is overshadowed on occasion.' However, George Perry noted rightly that when compared to Costner's more reserved Robin, Alan Rickman's performance came 'close to unbalancing the picture'.

As predicted, the British public embraced *Prince of Thieves* with open arms, flocking to see a film whose recommendation, as in the United States, was strictly by word of mouth. The film's makers promised 'a magical, medieval tale of yore' which was also a Robin Hood updated for the 1990s in the style of *Indiana Jones*. Even the banal theme song with the ungrammatical title – '(Everything I Do) I Do It For You' – remained at the top of the British Top 40 Singles Chart for a record-breaking 16 weeks.

So why should the critics dismiss a film that the public so obviously loved? Costner believed that it was his success in *Dances With Wolves* which signalled the change in critical attention. After all, until he had swept away the Oscars earlier that year, he had always enjoyed glowing appraisals of his work: 'I think I became a target about the same time as the Academy Awards. Like everybody, I went through life thinking I was immune to that stuff, but I'm not.'

Kevin and Cindy Costner attend
the celebrity premiere of *Robin
Hood: Prince Of Thieves* in 1991
with co-star Mary Elizabeth
Mastrantonio. She was a last-
minute replacement for the actress
Robin Wright.

True to the 800-year-old legend, the story
is set at the time of the Crusades. The film
opens in the Holy Land in 1194, in a Saracen
dungeon. Chained hand and foot to a wall,
his bedraggled appearance echoing his grim
predicament, the young English nobleman
Robin of Locksley (Costner) looks doomed
to die there. But seizing an opportunity, he
leads the other prisoners to revolt and
manages to escape with the help of a Moor

called Azeem (Morgan Freeman).

Returning home to England, Robin
discovers that during King Richard's absence,
the kingdom has fallen into the hands of the
evil Sheriff of Nottingham (Alan Rickman)
and his henchmen who have plundered the
country and reduced its population to
starving beggars. Robin learns that while he
was abroad his father Lord Locksley (Brian
Blessed) was wrongfully accused of devil-
worship and treason and slain by the Sheriff.
Angry, Robin vows to avenge his father's
murder and reclaim his confiscated lands.
But Robin clashes with some of the Sheriff's
men, killing several of them in battle. Forced
to flee, he hides out in Sherwood Forest
where he has the classic encounter with Little

John (Nick Brimble) and his rabble. Robin then joins up with the 'merry men', assorted adventures follow, until finally they foil the Sheriff's plans to take over the throne.

At 138 minutes in length, the film is, to say the least, over-stretched and bloated and hampered even more so by audiences knowing exactly what is going to happen next as the traditional story unfolds. But what it lacks in suspense, it certainly makes up for in action, helped along by a witty script. It is obvious that the film tries hard to be different from other Robin Hood tales, but doesn't quite make it. Costner's Robin is seen as both sensitive and sentimental, for instance, and even weeps in one scene. There are heavy overtones of Vietnam laid on to the part of the story describing the trauma experienced both by himself and his father when Robin returns from the Crusades to find his whole world changed. Costner explained the reason for the gritty realism of this remake of the 1938 Warner Brothers classic, *The Adventures of Robin Hood*: 'He was captured and held for five years, so he wasn't the carefree young rascal Errol Flynn was.'

The Errol Flynn version was Costner's favourite. 'By the time I was watching that film on TV it must have been around 25 years old. But it was still terrific,' he said. 'I admire Errol Flynn for being so good in such a silly movie.' Critics took great delight in comparing his performance unfavourably with Flynn's. 'As Robin,' wrote Ian Lyness in *The Daily Express,* 'Costner has the integrity of an athletic Gary Cooper rather than the devil-may-care panache of an Errol Flynn.' *Variety* wrote that Costner 'offers nothing comparable to the vigour and contagious enthusiasm of Errol Flynn in rallying his

men to the cause. Pic has little chance of coming electrifyingly to life as a result.'

Costner remained unperturbed by these jibes. 'I have tried to put my own stamp on this new version. What I saw in this script was a big sense of adventure as different to every previous version as could be, considering the tired story. The fresh originality in the writing helps the genre take a major leap...[suggesting] Robin was the first terrorist. He is not someone who has lived only in Sherwood Forest with a narrow view. He has seen real death and gore, and the true face of the Crusades.'

It was predictable that the introduction of a new black Muslim sidekick for Robin would result in the obligatory Hollywood wise-cracking black/white cop/buddy construct for the duo (Robin's preaching about racial prejudice drove some critics to denounce the film as 'so politically correct'). Although Mary Elizabeth Mastrantonio's stubbornly feminist Marion was a delight to watch, it was hardly a new idea. The 1950s' British television series *The Adventures of Robin Hood*, starring Richard Greene as Robin, had actress Patricia Driscoll frequently disguising herself as a man to join the action, while Tony Robinson (best known as Baldrick in the 'Blackadder' series) created a hilarious version of Robin Hood for children's TV in 1989 in which Marion was the leader of the gang and Robin merely a pathetic wimp.

For all its faults, however, *Prince of Thieves* still provides a mix of rousing battles, romance and laughs. A particularly arresting moment is when an unbilled Sean Connery shows up in a surprise cameo appearance at the end as King Richard I to give his blessing to Robin and Marion's marriage. The $400,000 fee paid to Connery for his one day's work was passed on by the star to his favourite cause, the Scottish Educational Trust.

Kevin Costner found it exciting to be filming a story he had loved ever since he was a boy. In a way it was quite fitting that his two biggest films to date, *Robin Hood* and *Dances With Wolves,* should pay homage to old movies. Robin Hood in particular has been constantly recycled since the birth of the movies, making his screen debut in a silent British film of 1909. This was followed in 1922 by *Robin Hood,* an elaborate Hollywood interpretation starring Douglas Fairbanks that was most notable for its exhilarating stunts and extravagant sets. As well as Errol Flynn's version of 1938, there have been four other movie versions, plus a Western version (*Robin Hood of El Dorado,* 1938). And there were at least two TV versions, the latest of which, *Robin of Sherwood,* starred Richard Praed and Sean Connery's son Jason.

Given that Robin Hood has scarcely been off the screen in 80 years, it was not surprising that there should be a revival of interest in filming further adventures of the popular and enduring character. But the sudden decision to mount three separate productions simultaneously must again be attributed to the conventional Hollywood 'wisdom' of copying sure-fire subject matter. John Irvin, director of the 20th Century Fox *Robin Hood* confirmed this: 'The majority of producers are looking for bandwagons. They're the last to actually *lead* – they're just good at jumping on and off.'

20th Century Fox claimed to be the first to come in with a Robin Hood remake, and

Irvin's superior, the Fox chairman Joe Roth, was less courteous about his colleagues. In *Variety* he accused the two rival studios – TriStar and Morgan Creek – of jumping on *his* bandwagon. Roth, who had recently announced his intentions to remake the Robin Hood story, felt that they had 'acted unjustly, if not immorally, by rushing competing Robin Hoods into production when Fox was first'.

Competition was stiff from the outset. 20th Century Fox's *Robin Hood,* starring Patrick Bergin as the outlaw and Uma Thurman as Marion, had already started shooting in Cheshire, England, by September 1990, ahead of its original October date. With Costner cast in the role for its version, Morgan Creek advanced their schedule to catch up, and at this point TriStar wisely pulled out altogether. Several stars had been in line for the starring role in their version. Mel Gibson had recently turned it down, worried that the period setting would be too similar to his almost-completed *Hamlet,* directed by Franco Zeffirelli, and the backers vetoed the director's choice of Kevin Kline, as they had reservations about his pulling power at the box office in competition with Costner. Costner himself had been offered the part in all three productions. 'I honestly don't know why that was,' he said afterwards. 'Do I look like Robin Hood?'

Either way, Morgan Creek executive producer James G. Robinson was clearly delighted that they had netted him. 'It was not vital to get a huge star, but to get a megastar like Kevin is great. We had the three top star actors in mind, but never had to go past Number One on the list.'

Filming began in England in late

September 1990. The long flight to London filled Costner with a series of conflicting emotions. A constant nagging fear that everything was not quite right had stayed with him since he had first signed the contract. His gut feeling, so often a deciding factor over his choice of scripts was flashing red. 'I'd originally passed it up,' he said, 'because I suspected the whole project hadn't been fully thought out.'

But he had given his word to the director, Kevin Reynolds. 'I only took the part after Kevin was hired as director,' he said. Kevin Reynolds had given him his first big break in *Fandango* when Costner was still an unknown, and he felt he owed it to him. Costner also knew they worked well together.

Yet he was still uncertain. For the first time since the beginning of his career, discounting the barren years stuck in the black hole of low-budget oblivion, the thought of filming a project his heart was not in had filled him with dread. He felt exhausted and drained. 'I was completely empty,' he said. *Dances With Wolves* had finished post-production work only four days earlier; the tremendous burden of having carried the film – not only as director/producer/star but also controller of the finances – still hung heavily on this shoulders. No one knew yet how well the film would be received. He wondered whether his stubbornness had finally caused him to overstep his mark. To add to his gloom, Costner's just released *Revenge* had flopped miserably at the box office. For once his over-abundant confidence had been shaken. He felt powerless, swept up in events that, for once, were going faster than he wanted them to. Had he made the wrong decision? He wondered whether he had broken his long-held rule and allowed personal feelings to cloud his judgment.

Arriving at Heathrow Airport from the warmth of his Californian home, Costner was greeted by typically dreary British autumn weather. Its unpredictability was to have a paralysing effect on the shoot. There was also an unwelcome reception committee of overly-aggressive, jostling *paparazzi* photographers determined to get the 'great shot' – regardless of the obvious discomfort this embarrassing attention focussed on the publicity-shy star.

He was taken by limousine straight to Shepperton Studios on the outskirts of London. It was pouring with rain, and if he had looked at his script at that point, no doubt the similarity of his predicament to the character Azeem in *Prince of Thieves* would not have escaped him. 'The hospitality in this country is as warm as the weather,' Azeem says to Robin as they arrive back in England to similar climatic conditions and an unfriendly reception.

Everything around the production was a shambles. It had been saddled with a gruelling 100-day schedule by the management at Morgan Creek. John Watson, producer and co-scriptwriter for the movie recounted the reasons for the disarray: 'Getting the film into production was a wild ride. Not only were we in a race with two other planned Robin Hood pictures but we knew we had to start filming in September so we could guarantee having leaves on our Sherwood Forest trees. I ended up in the extraordinary situation of hiring the production designer and other Heads of Department before we had decided on our director.

Fortunately Kevin Reynolds loved my choices and we were able to start on time.'

Despite the initial struggle to get things moving quickly, there were more setbacks to come. Robin Wright, original choice as Maid Marion, had to relinquish her role after she became pregnant by her boyfriend Sean Penn. With producers in a panic, and casting agents despatched to Hollywood to find a replacement, *Abyss* star Mary Elizabeth Mastrantonio was eventually offered the job four days before shooting was due to begin.

Costume designer John Bloomfield was not so fortunate. Given just 24 hours' notice to replace the original wardrobe man, whose services Reynolds had described as 'most unsatisfactory', he was still up to his elbows in fabrics on the very eve of the first day's filming. 'We were working on the costumes for Kevin Costner and Morgan Freeman until three in the morning and were due 100 miles away in Eastbourne [for a location shoot] at 5.30am. We got straight into a car, drove through the night and put the costumes on their backs. If we hadn't been so far behind, I think we would have been sacked on the spot.'

According to Costner, however, Bloomfield and his team of harried workers had managed to retain some humour. 'I was worried about having to wear green tights like Errol Flynn and so, as a joke on the first day, the costume department laid out a neat little green tunic, a green hat with a feather, and of course, the green tights! I burst out laughing and fortunately that set of clothes was quickly put back into storage.'

Indeed much was made of the mainly male cast's reluctance to slip into the traditional Forest fatigues. Costner's rebellious comrade Will Scarlett, played by the young American actor Christian Slater, was having none of it either. Speaking to a journalist in an interview prior to the film's release, he said: 'I was so thrilled when I read in a magazine that Kevin said he's not wearing tights. I definitely want to stress that I am *not* wearing any tights either! Make sure you put it in the story so I get the message across. You read it here – **no tights**.'

Kevin Costner, too, was not immune to the problems of the shortened schedule. He found his promised rehearsal time had been revoked, 'I went into making the film with my eyes open and I knew we were going to go very quickly. Some of the things that I thought were going to take place didn't and that caused a lot of problems to me personally... It's important for me to give a good show, which means you need to practice, you need to rehearse, it needs all these things to make for good movies, only we weren't able to afford that time on this film.'

By the middle of December, the production was four weeks behind schedule. Kevin Reynolds was furious. 'We wanted the English look, we wanted that drizzle. And we paid a price for it... Only six hours of daylight. It's...*horrible.*'

Another major problem was Costner's apparent inability to pick up a convincing English accent. With the race against time nearly over, James G. Robinson of Morgan Creek stepped in and sacked Costner's voice coach. 'Hell, have Kevin play Kevin Costner,' he barked. 'We'll fix it at dubbing stage.'

When questioned on the subject at a later date, co-producer John Watson said diplomatically: 'We have an interesting blend of British and American voices, which I think will be accepted when people hear them. We have asked dialogue coaches to soften American accents, without making them sound English. I think it's something that will only be noticed in the United Kingdom.'

Costner himself felt it was not important to have an 'authentic' English accent. 'The way people are talking in England today is certainly not the way they were talking 500 years ago, so who's to know what's right?' he said. On the other hand, the film had a predominantly English cast, so he tried to develop what he called a 'soft English accent', to blend in with the others and not draw attention to himself.

Costner made up for his vocal inadequacies in the action scenes, insisting on doing his own stunts, much to the consternation of the production team. 'They tried stopping me because of insurance when I did *Silverado*,' he said. 'They didn't stop me then and now they definitely can't...because now I'm too successful to take orders.' In a more serious mood, Costner has said: 'I don't have a death wish. I won't do something I don't think I can handle or something that doesn't have to be me.' He added: 'But if I can't see anyone doing it better than me then I put myself in the shot. I'm that kind of guy. Action is something I identify with a lot. If there's something in my way I'll run through it, I'll jump over it, I'll do what I think the normal guy would do in that situation.'

Throughout the shoot Costner kept a team of stuntmen idle as he avidly duelled with quarterstaffs (getting dunked repeatedly in near-freezing water), flew Tarzan-like on a burning rope from tree to tree 40 feet above the ground, and teetered on the spray-splashed prow of a tiny insecure wooden boat

Kevin Costner glimpsed on location during the shooting of *Robin Hood: Prince of Thieves*. The break-neck speed of the shooting schedule strained the long-time friendship between Costner and his director Kevin Reynolds.

during a storm. Of the scene shot in raging seas beneath the Seven Sisters cliffs near Eastbourne, Costner declared: 'It was probably the most dangerous thing I've ever done in a movie. I had such heavy clothes on that, if I'd fallen overboard, I'd have drowned.'

But he seemed to thrive on danger. He laughed off the concern shown by others at the life-threatening risks he took, claiming that concentration and attention prevented accidents from happening. 'I'm a bit of a running-and-jumping actor,' he has said. Perhaps more revealingly, he added: 'I enjoyed the boys' stuff involved in this movie.' But he admitted that the hardest part was the fight with Little John in freezing water, which took four days to shoot.

Kevin Costner's single-minded quest for perfection and close attention to detail were blamed for the endless numbers of retakes which slowed down the shoot. Nick Brimble, the 6ft 4in British actor who played Little John was both frustrated and amazed at the lengths Costner would go to get the best possible shot. During the fight scene with eight foot quarterstaffs, filmed at Aysgarth Falls in North Yorkshire, Costner begged Brimble over and over again to hit him really hard.

Distraught, soaked with water, his body would sag. Again and again Brimble would raise the huge quarterstaff above his shoulders. Costner would exhale wearily, biting his lip, as he steeled himself for the crushing blows. And so the takes would continue, the stars toppling over, forcing each other to take another dip in the treacherous torrent. Brimble later remarked: 'A lot of things have been said about Costner but one thing I can tell you – he's not afraid of getting hurt. We

were both covered in cuts and bruises and risked breaking our legs throughout the shot.'

Cindy Costner, relieved when the river scenes were finally over, revealed to a journalist when she flew in to join her husband, how he was 'really scared to go back in the water' and that he would lie awake at night dreading the next day. She described how one morning Kevin was awakened from a dreamless sleep by the sound of his alarm call at 6.30am. He had fumbled for the light, knocking the phone over in his confusion. He was disorientated with fatigue: instead of the familiar surroundings of his home, he was in a strange bedroom. He had been awake till four in the morning worrying about the shoot. And every night was the same.

Up until this point, the stunt co-ordinator, Paul Weston, had shown incredible tolerance towards Costner. But he could bear it no longer. He took the actor to one side. 'I had to tell him, "It's not worth putting yourself into a situation where you can be badly injured. It's not good for you, not good for the film and it's not safe for the others around".'

But it was not only daring deeds that Costner had to contend with. Mike McShane, the boisterous American-born comedian best known to British audiences for his improvisations in *Whose Line Is It Anyway?*, relished his role as Friar Tuck. 'I get to kick Kevin in the face and wrestle him to the ground while he begs me to let go. Then I bite his leg!' was how he described it.

Perfection was what Costner demanded. But the more he pushed himself to the limit, the further he alienated himself from the cast and crew. He made few friends on the shoot, preferring to keep to himself in his trailer, or hiding away in the sanctuary of his hotel suite. 'I don't generally hang with anybody on the set,' he said. 'I'm kind of like the guy who likes to get letters but doesn't like to write. I like to be with people, but I don't have to be, I don't know what that makes me.'

As a star who had become accustomed to getting his own way on the set, Costner had displayed what some critics had described as something close to 'egomaniacal behaviour' on occasion, earning him uncomplimentary comparisons with Orson Welles. Kevin's co-star Morgan Freeman disagreed with the assumptions: 'Kevin's giving, he's real, he's there, he's honest, he's available. If you're working with an actor, you don't want to hear, "Just a second", when you need to talk to him. You've got Kevin's immediate attention. There's no in-between people separating the lord and master from the great unwashed. He's one guy who's taken his success in stride.'

To add to his growing discontent on the set, Costner's long-standing friendship with Kevin Reynolds had become severely strained. Constantly at odds with each other, with disparate opinions about how they saw the film, heated arguments ensued. At one point, Costner actually took the second unit off to re-shoot a key scene (Robin's home-coming from the Crusades) – this time directing himself and leaving Kevin Reynolds to finish other scenes the star didn't feature in.

Asked to explain this, Costner insisted he was merely returning a favour to Reynolds who had shot three weeks of second unit for

him on *Dances With Wolves*. 'I *have* a reputation,' he shrugged. 'But every director I have worked with has asked to work with me again. We have combative things. What they feel at the end of the day is that the arguments are about the movie and not other things. They are *not* about who is the most important person on set or the decoration in my trailer. My problems exist only about the behaviour of the movie itself.

'For as much money as actors earn today, they should care about their work and sweat about details. They should worry when things aren't right.'

Later, on reflection, and when the film was completed, Costner would partially contradict his earlier remarks. 'We were like little boys in a world that gets very big and complicated. I think it's been a painful process for both of us.'

Right from the word go Reynolds had been under no illusions why he had been given the director's job. With two less than startling movies in the last ten years to his credit, including 1988's *The Beast*, he believed it was his close friendship with Costner that had won the backers over. Why else would the film company risk $60 million to a director who had minimal box office success? 'Did Morgan Creek know that Kevin would be more interested in working with me, as a friend, than with Fox?' he asked bitterly. 'I don't know – they probably did. Did they hire me because they wanted to lure Kevin away from the Fox project? I don't know – they probably did. I'll never know. Whatever, it worked, if that *was* their purpose.'

Reynolds is reputed to have walked off the production at the editing stage, disgruntled with the powers-that-be tampering with his

almost completed work. 'Kevin Reynolds was essentially told to distance himself,' Douglas Milsome, the Director of Photography told *Vanity Fair*. 'When I tried to get into the cutting room to colour-grade the picture, I was never able to see all of it. They – whoever "they" were – wouldn't let me. But Costner was in the cutting room, playing with his part, putting more close-ups of himself in, which Reynolds had left out.'

Costner was well aware that he had left himself open to criticism by supporting the producers' decision to hedge out Reynolds. Credited as 'Production Consultant' on the finished movie, Costner said during the editing process, 'If this movie has any trouble later on, what a nice angle: "Kevin Costner took the reins and started directing himself." This monster!'

Kevin Reynolds' worst fears were confirmed when he was finally allowed to see the new results. 'I thought that in a number of places the changes to the film were pretty awkward and embarrassing,' he said. Reynolds failed to attend the celebrity premiere of his film, and it is said that the two Kevins became estranged. 'I have to say our friendship's not what it once was,' Reynolds admitted in January 1992. 'I'm really sorry we're not as close as we were. You'd think that someone that's a friend would respect you enough as a filmmaker not to try to interfere with what you're trying to do. I haven't talked to him for several months.'

Costner too was clearly upset with the moguls at Morgan Creek. 'You know, I don't think the producers of this movie answer every question that's thrown at them, they're trying to make the picture sound like it was all rosy. That's bullshit, that's a lie. And if I could go back again I wouldn't make the movie again. Not because it's not any good, but because environment is important to me.'

The star was further antagonised when the infamous Robin 'nude' scene was first revealed. Although Costner had previously allowed his nude back view to be revealed both in *Revenge* and *Dances With Wolves* he had a body-double stand in for him during the nude bathing scene which was also shot at Aysgarth Falls. Angry that the clip had featured in the film trailer, he accused the production company of cheekily playing up the scene to attract female fans.

'I feel used,' he complained. 'I agreed to the swimming scene because it was important to the original script. But the meaning of the nudity was left on the cutting room floor. It seems it was just an opportunity to titillate.'

But it wasn't just about titillation, it was about control and Costner felt he lacked it after the total control he exercised over *Dances With Wolves*. 'I liked having my own control in that film,' he explained. 'I could relax. Control is not having to worry about anything. If I was under the influence of people they would say: "Do it this way or that way." But I want it to be really up to me.' By the time *Prince of Thieves* was released in the summer of 1991, *Dances With Wolves* had achieved its runaway success and Costner felt, with reason, that he was being exploited because the production company had tried to capitalize on his status.

Costner was angry and showed it. The mild-mannered man was showing his teeth. But it was merely a foretaste of what was to come.

Chapter Six

American Flyer

WHEN Kevin Costner returned to the USA in early 1991 having completed filming on *Robin Hood: Prince Of Thieves*, he was greeted by a storm of controversy regarding his alleged liaisons with other women. The storm had been whipped up by a series of reports in the British tabloid press, and for Costner now all hell had broken loose. Although he had returned to twelve Academy Award nominations for *Dances With Wolves*, he was also fighting desperately to save his marriage from collapsing.

The star, who had said that the only woman he felt truly comfortable with was his

Costner carrying Lily and Joe, his younger children. A caring family man, he has admitted to feeling guilty because he doesn't spend as much time as he would like to with his wife and children.

wife Cindy, was at the centre of a scandal when Sheri Stewart – an employee of Stringfellows nightclub in London – alleged in the British Sunday tabloid the *News Of The World* that she'd had a fling ('Costner Was A Wolf In My Bed!') with Kevin while he was in England filming *Prince Of Thieves*. Ms Stewart, 27, claimed that Costner had invited her back to his London hotel. There, she confessed: 'He made love with such passion he brought tears to my eyes.'

Costner (who had said in 1988: 'As yet the gossip writers haven't linked me with anyone. I know they will at a certain point and that will be hurtful'), refused to be drawn on the subject. In private, he was furious but he tried to carry on as normal.

Shortly afterwards, in April, Costner was at the centre of a new scandal when an American bit-part actress, Christine Dinard, then aged 32, accused the star of using bully tactics to prevent her talking about the secret relationship they had allegedly shared for eleven years, right from the time when Kevin was a struggling young actor. But silenced no longer, and speaking exclusively to the British Sunday tabloid *The People*, Dinard declared: 'He said his marriage was back on track and his career was making great strides. I was happy for him but underneath he was saying, "I don't need you anymore." Eventually Kevin turned to me and admitted it.'

Costner reacted angrily: 'I've made no secret of my struggles in the past,' he said bitterly, 'but to comment on any of these things is to give them credibility. There's always going to be rumours and gossip. I suppose I just have to live with that.'

Reiterating the dismay he felt when critics panned *Prince Of Thieves*, Costner complained at the way people expected him to pay for his success. 'They put you up there,' he said, 'and then sit back and wait to see your marriage collapse or drugs destroy you or some other terrible thing. Then they will be able to say "Kevin had too much success too early and now he's finally paying for it."' He explained that he had not gone into acting lightly and that his parents had worried that it was going to be very tough, knowing that the odds against success were staggering. 'What they didn't know – and what I could never have guessed – is that however successful you become there are still things that are going to hurt,' added Costner. With regard to his relationship with Cindy, he went on to explain: 'We don't have a perfect marriage by any means but we do work at it. People are surprised our marriage works. It seems as if they wish it didn't.'

If Costner was determined to hold his shaky marriage together, then so was his wife Cindy. Fighting back against the accusations of her husband's infidelity, she drew up a four-point plan to save their marriage. 'Since Kevin became recognised on a worldwide scale there have been difficulties,' she admitted. She described the numerous reports in both the US and British press that he was continually having wild affairs. Since she was anxious to stop their marriage falling apart, she had decided to come up with a plan to save it. 'I sat Kevin down,' she said, 'and told him – and he agreed to everything. Now we're more in love than ever and our kids are happy as clams.'

The plan that Cindy had drawn up stipulated the following four points – that the family should be committed to living in their new home; that Cindy and the children should go on location with Kevin; that the family should find a 'getaway place' to be alone; and finally, that Cindy and Kevin should be honest with each other. From now on the Costners would have to work hard to put Cindy's 'plan' into action.

For eight years, since 1983, the Costners had lived in the same small house in the North Hollywood suburb of La Canada. But the family have since moved into a $1 million Mediterranean-style villa 50 miles outside Hollywood in Glendale, a remote neighbourhood partly hidden by fir-tree covered hills. Designed by that same architect for whom Costner once worked ('One day you're gonna help me build a house just like this!' the young Costner had said, admiringly, as he stood on the veranda of an Italianate villa they had been contracted to renovate. 'Yes ...' laughed his friend, 'but let's get this job

Costner cycles round the *Silverado* set with Cindy and their first child, Annie, in 1984. There had been a time when a bicycle was their only form of transport.

finished first!'), it reportedly took a team of builders almost four years to construct the five-bedroomed house complete with swimming pool, tennis and basketball courts.

The garage held more bicycles than anything else – the family cars consisted of a '68 Shelby Mustang (licence plate: CRASH D, for his *Bull Durham* character), that Costner drove during the week and a multi-seated Bronco van for outings at the weekends. 'It's difficult for us to go out because I get asked for autographs all the time,' Costner explained, which was also the reason for the huge 15ft walls that surrounded the sprawling grounds. 'People haven't started

bothering me at the grocery, which is a good thing because I insist on going,' he added. 'I don't want to become a recluse, and, with three kids, sometimes my wife can't go. So I have to help out.' However keen he may have been to protect his anonymity from over-zealous fans, Costner has always been happy to entertain the family's friends. 'I like the way we live,' he said in 1991. 'Our Danish nanny – who's been with us for four years – has all her friends over to stay too. Our kids' friends are also always around. That's the way I'm comfortable.'

Cindy's second stipulation – that the family should accompany Costner on location – is perhaps more difficult to understand because of the disruption caused to the children's lives. Not only did she and the children, who were seven, five, and three at the time, fly over to join Costner in London while he was filming *Prince Of Thieves*, but they were even cast as extras on *Dances With Wolves*. From Costner's point of view it's hard not to think that having Cindy and the children around him on the set could be distracting for the actor, leading to friction between him and his wife. Costner has offered a clue to this: 'It's weird,' he has said, 'you sometimes find yourself thinking: "I could do this better if I was by myself".' So the price you pay for not being alone is there, but there's this other thing – experiencing your family – that you can never put a price on.'

To his credit, Kevin has always helped out with the raising of his children. 'When Annie was born, Cindy went right back to work and I took care of her for the first two, three months,' he has said. 'It was hard but I loved it. I took her to my meetings, sometimes some pretty high-level ones, I'd say, "Can you turn your phones down a little bit?... They're waking up my kid". And if Annie needed care, if her diaper needed changing – the meeting came to a halt. We didn't realise how great she was until Lily came along. She gets up whenever she wants and she's not regular at all. But they're both smilers.'

Costner's film contracts now stipulate that not only his wife and children, but also his in-laws can join him on location. This image of the happy family man trying to juggle both interests, whilst at the same time striving to

maintain a mutually satisfying harmony, can easily appear on the outside to be quite commendable; however at times Costner has admitted to something of a Jekyll-and-Hyde existence, commenting that when his family comes to the set, he has a lot of fun with the kids. 'But then there's the side that I can't fully explain. It's almost like being drunk. When I talk about a dark side it's just that I'm not that good. But I'm not that bad either – I'm not a heroin addict or anything. It's just that when you play heroes you are expected to behave like one all the time.'

Cindy's third stipulation was that she and Kevin should find a getaway place, where they could be alone. Granted their Glendale home offered seclusion, away from prying eyes, but they were unable to step outside the gates without causing a commotion. 'I went

Costner allowed himself to be designated 'Man of the Year' in 1990 by the Hasty Puddings Theatricals of Harvard, a well-known student drag event.

to Alaska and there were 30 people waiting for me,' Costner complained. 'I couldn't even go unnoticed in somewhere like Alaska!' The Costners had perhaps become prisoners of Kevin's fame. Kevin has said that he is at his most comfortable amongst friends and family – in other words, in a 'crowd'. Left at home, and alone for weeks on end, then having to share their 'catching up' time with others, was it any wonder Cindy felt neglected? The big question then, was where would they go to escape? Crowd-seeker, perhaps, but Kevin was resolute about where he would not go: 'I don't spend a lot of time with the fringe benefits of my business,' he has asserted. 'I'm not at Steamboat Springs for a week of celebrity skiing. It's not that I don't think that would be fun, but that's not a part of my program. I'm not immune to the perks of celebrity, I just don't have a lot of time for them.' Admittedly, the Costners also had a condo in the High Sierras and a beach house in Santa Barbara – but with three young children under the age of eight at the time, there was not much chance of being alone in the first place, never mind getting away.

Cindy's final requirement was honesty. 'Ultimately,' she said, 'Kevin has to tell me once in a while that ours is the greatest love story ever.'

'I would really be disappointed with myself if our relationship blew up, if I couldn't do these films and keep my marriage together, too,' Kevin said. 'Cindy was there at the beginning and we're just as much a team now as then.' Costner added that he did not care if he was deemed a good actor, but that for him keeping his marriage together was truly a worthwhile accomplishment. He went

on to explain that by this time, in 1991, Cindy and he had been together for fifteen years and were prepared to solve any problems that had come up. 'The hazards really begin as opportunities, and it's then down to what you do with it, both in your career and your private life.'

Much has been said and written about Kevin's alleged affairs, but what about his other liaisons, on-screen? One might imagine that for Cindy, the sight of her husband in the throes of ecstasy, consumed with passion, making love to other women, must be hard to take, even if it is 'only acting'. 'It's not easy for her,' Kevin agreed. 'The children wonder why it's not their mother and, naturally, Cindy's very glad it's just a movie. She can look at it as my job – up to a point – then she has to look at it as a woman.' He continued: 'Most people think about all the beautiful women you come into contact with. But it works the other way too. I have had my share of the world's beautiful women on the screen, so I have been able to live out a lot of my fantasies in my work.' He went on to explain how much he loved the company of women, but above all, 'I love coming home to a woman who appreciates how truly full of baloney I am.' He added: 'If things were reversed it would be impossible. That's how strong Cindy is. I don't think I could do what she does.'

For a star who can currently command $8 million a movie, Costner can still remember the difficult times when all they had between them was $13. 'Cindy and I have gone through too much together to forget those days,' he said.

It is impossible to say how big a part Cindy Costner has had in her husband's success, but there is no doubt that she has been a rock to lean on at times in his life, a calming influence on his brash, impulsive nature. Not content to lounge around swank Beverly Hills salons all day, swapping 'juicy' gossip, as Jackie Collins would have us believe, Cindy has never intended becoming a 'Hollywood wife', an opinion confirmed by Costner's elder brother and financial adviser, Dan: 'She's active, she's involved.' Cindy's brother David Silva, an assistant director on *Dances With Wolves*, admits that the enormous pressures of Kevin's success have put a strain on the Costners' relationship. 'I know it wasn't easy at the beginning,' he commented. 'But I think she's grown with it real well. She's an amazing person. She's kind of a wedge. She fits into any situation. She's been a good wife to Kevin. It's got to be tough on the spouse. This business is such an emotional roller coaster. It's bigger than life and the stakes are high.'

'They've already weathered a hell of a lot,' testifies Costner's close friend Michael Blake, the author of *Dances With Wolves*. 'Just the fact that they're still together says a lot about their union. Kevin is extremely conservative, and he doesn't believe in breaking up, no matter what.'

But Costner has admitted his marriage is not perfect. 'It's just like anybody else. We have those long drives home, like everybody does, where there are silences that are uncomfortable,' he has said. 'Then there are other days when we think how lucky we are.' But Costner claimed not to have the secret for a successful marriage: 'I don't want to take a title – like America's Couple – that sets me up as someone who has,' and understood that if his marriage failed people would blame

his career: 'People are going to point to show business as the problem, and it's not.' Undoubtedly Kevin has realised that 'To succeed in a relationship you need a lot of luck, a lot of maturity, and then a lot more luck in order to keep it all together.'

All his life Costner has tried to live by the same kind of standards he saw in his father: hard working, honest, fair. Now that he has children of his own, he has tried to instil in them those same old-fashioned values. 'I want my kids to think of me as I think of Spencer Tracy,' he told Lester Middlehurst, showbusiness writer for the British tabloid *Today*, 'because that's how I think of my dad. I'm not as good as the characters I've played and I'm not as strong as them, but I do my best. That's what I want my kids to know.'

Costner continued: 'I think I'm a good dad – when I'm at home. Sometimes the only way I can spend time with my kids is when I cast them in my movies. But I bet I see them more than most nine-to-five dads.' Costner explained how they came on location when it was possible and he would take care of them when he was not working. 'Cindy and I talk a lot about raising our kids. I want them to like being with their family and doing things with us, like I did with my dad – hunting, fishing together.' Like many families, the Costners enjoy fishing and have a boat, they also love swimming and going off for picnics.

Costner has admitted that he feels guilty that he cannot be with his family every day: 'I try to get home each night to tuck the kids into bed. Or home for dinner with them after work, like my dad always was.' He described how his children are involved in sports so he has tried to see all their kickball games, or help his daughters get ready for Girl Scouts,

Costner with Cindy, the children and their nanny in London, during the shooting of *Robin Hood*. The difficulties of his time in Britain subsequently brought the family closer together.

so they have 'a dad they remember'. 'When I'm away,' he added, 'my hotel-room walls are lined with pictures of my family. But I try not to spoil them. It can be rough at times but I'm determined that my family is going to live as normal a life as possible.' He explained how he felt when limousines came to pick the family up: 'Are they gonna think they're entitled to that for the rest of their lives? I've gotta be their parent,' he added. 'That's the most important thing. I'm not responsible for their behaviour for the rest of their lives, but I have to be there for them now to tell them when they please me and why.' Costner explained that what was important to him was the kind of people his children became. 'You always worry the hell about them. It's a burden too – a bittersweet kind of thing.'

He went on to say: 'I know I can do better with relationships with my family, and I have to figure out how. There's just not enough time for the people I care about.' Costner described how he separated things in order to maintain both his public and private lives: I don't want to stop what I'm doing, and I don't want to lose what I have.'

Although Costner tried to retain this simple, down-to-earth approach in his life, with huge, multi-million dollar pay cheques constantly on the increase, by 1992 he reached the enviable position of naming his price for any future films. The big question was whether he could keep things in proportion. 'I still consider myself a very average person who makes a really extraordinary income,' he explained. 'I have to pinch myself occasionally but I try not to dwell on money. I wake up really happy about my family. I'm doing exactly what I want to do.

Costner shares a joke with Joel McCrea in Los Angeles, April, 1989. McCrea is one of the few survivors among Hollywood's great male stars admired by Costner, men like Gary Cooper, James Stewart and Gregory Peck, who represent a golden age of movie-making to the younger star.

We used to have to save and it was a very big deal to get things. But because of the amount of money I now make we don't have to wait for things any more. If we fancy something then we have it.

'But I would trade much to get back my anonymity,' he added solemnly.

'If I get a million dollars for a film, I like to think that I get $100,000 for the acting and the other $900,000 for my loss of privacy. That is something I'll never, ever get back.'

Costner has been portrayed as a shrewd, sometimes ruthless business man whose college training in business studies stood him in good stead once his estimated personal fortune was said to be in excess of $100 million. His business acumen has been put to the test when hammering out contracts, but in fact a large role was also played by his elder brother Dan.

Dan Costner, head of finances at Costner's Tig Productions (called after their grandmother's nickname), has been an investor and became a millionaire in his own right. Kevin brought his brother in to deal with his multi-million dollar empire, and Dan has invested wisely for his brother in a variety of ways, ranging from property and land, to small businesses and shares in other companies. In 1991 the Costners purchased a South Dakota casino, called The Midnight

Star, complete with fruit machines, card tables and roulette, with Kevin retaining his 'anonymity', as silent partner. And around the time of *Robin Hood*, he showed that he wasn't too proud to cash in on the merchandising potential of the role, with an Action-Man style doll complete with longbow.

Kevin Costner will always be, in his own words, something of an enigma: 'If you say what you mean in this town, you're an outlaw. You know you're on the right track if Hollywood finds you an enigma.' When asked by one journalist if the success of *Dances With Wolves* had given him power, he snapped: 'I've always had power – what's bad is that I don't need the attention. I don't need the fame, it doesn't serve me in any capacity, it doesn't help me to go to work in the morning.'

James Earl Jones, Costner's co-star in *Field Of Dreams*, said: 'Everyone respects power in this business and Kevin's is a unique brand of power. It's not predictable. He's not after mega-millions or making sure his ego is fulfilled. He isn't macho, he's pure male. If you press the wrong button the man is dangerous. He won't explode – that's counter productive – but he will set you straight real fast.'

'Kevin's an enormous force in the industry,' said Jim Wilson, Costner's closest friend and his partner in Tig Productions. 'He understands the clout he has, and he's going to use it.'

This power, added Susan Sarandon who starred alongside Costner in *Bull Durham*, has been earned the hard way. 'He's paid his dues. He's had a while to figure out who he is and what he's about and what he stands for. He also really understands how the industry works, so he can sit down with the power brokers and hold his own and see what games they're playing.' She concluded: 'He's very smart that way.'

'Quite simply – Kevin can do it all,' confirmed Casey Silver, president of world-wide production for the MCA Motion Picture Group, former owners of Universal Studios for which Costner made Steven Spielberg's *Amazing Stories*.

But Costner does not intend to rest on his laurels. 'If the adulation you get from being successful in movies is your main reason for living, you won't ever be satisfied. That can't sustain you.'

What sustains Costner, he has said, is the knowledge that he's chosen the right project. He refuses to be restricted to what is 'hot' at the moment – whether it be 'buddy-buddy' cop movies or serial-killer thrillers. Costner has even said that he would do five westerns in a row, if the scripts were good enough. 'I've given up trying to predict success for my pictures. I've refused to stifle myself creatively by worrying what may, or may not, happen.'

For him the important thing has always been the need for a tautly-written script – 'carefully crafted stories, heavy with emotion, strong characters and a believable outcome.' He has expressed his great admiration for the work of directors such as Steven Spielberg, Lawrence Kasdan, Bernardo Bertolucci and John Ford, while he frowns upon what he calls the 'New-Age' breed of film-makers. 'All the camera work in the world can't disguise that there's no story – my movies can't be salvaged by a car chase.'

Costner has explained that he does not make films as 'personal Valentines'. 'I like to share the movies with as many people as will find them,' he said. 'I'm not necessarily trying to please people, but I'm not in the business of trying to confuse 'em either. I prefer to think of myself as...perhaps being not altogether predictable.'

How about approachable then? Strolling through the city centre in Atlanta, Georgia, taking a well-earned opportunity to escape from the rigours of the *Bull Durham* set by going shopping, Costner asked a *Rolling Stone* reporter who'd joined him for the day: 'You walked around in K-Mart with me ... Did anybody say a fucking word to me? I just go where I want to go.' But as the reporter wryly noted, 'He was hiding behind huge dark shades'.

Contrary to certain press reports, Costner has always been happy to sign autographs, pose for photographs, or simply stand and chat on set. While his privacy away from filming is precious to him, recognition while on location has always been part of the job for stars. 'The things that come of it are always nice,' he said. 'I get a lot of fringe benefits. I think people genuinely want to show you their city. They treat me the way I've always wanted to be treated in life, which is with a lot of graciousness. The only problem I ever have is with drunks. They dominate your time. I told you the up side, but there is a down side. I don't handle it very well. I don't usually blow them off, but I'm really disgusted when I let somebody dominate my time. I'm also aware that if I do something, it can create a scene.' As Costner has warned, 'I can be pushed about a hundred yards, but there's one inch that's really mine, and it's not a great idea for anybody to get in there. I'm kind of afraid of that ugly streak.'

'People look at me and think they see everything,' Costner has protested. 'But what they see is one moment frozen in time. I've come from somewhere to get to that point. There's stuff in my back pockets or up my sleeves that they don't know anything about. Generally people want to know more about me than they want to reveal about themselves. So of course I hold back.'

Costner went on to explain how show business really encourages a 'talk-show' mentality. 'You've got 15 minutes to be as charming as you can to the millions who are watching. But we all know that's not the real measure of someone. The morning after the show, you've got to get up and work all day with the people who get to see what you're really like.'

A mystery, not least to himself, Costner also hates to be tagged. 'People put these kinds of titles on you. The Risk Taker. The Perfect Husband. Those are labels and I don't like them. The risks I take in this business are personal, not professional. Professionally, I will always be able to go on and make another movie. Personally, I just don't want to make a bad movie.'

But this was 1991, and lurking in the background were the bad movies Costner had already made. *Shadows Run Black* and *Sizzle Beach, USA*, the two low-budget movies he made at the beginning of his career in the late 'seventies, had re-surfaced to 'coincide' with the success of *Dances With Wolves* at the Oscars that year. Along with them came the newspaper revelations: 'Costner fury at films he doesn't want you to see.' Described in the press as 'soft porn romps', it was reported that Costner had 'approached' film boss Eric Louzil apparently with a view to buying the rights to the films, thereby securing their rightful place in the dustbin of naivety. But Louzil had already sold the movies to a distribution company, and they eventually turned up for sale on video tape at the Cannes Film Festival in May that year. Clarke Kaufman, head of Troma Films who made the movies, even offered Costner an all-expenses paid trip to the French Riviera to promote the films. At the time they were made, 'Kevin was just another male bimbo on the block with a lot of ambition,' he said. 'He's made it big and now we're making a lot of money out of him.' He added: 'Kevin's people didn't seem at all keen. It's a shame he can't see the funny side of it.'

Straight after receiving a Golden Apple award, Kevin Costner talks to fans on his way in to the premiere of Hook.

Reluctant to talk about it in great detail, Costner offered this explanation about the sexploitation movies that he said 'had tit or ass every six minutes but weren't porn'. He explained: 'My acting teacher asked me if I wanted to do a role and I said, "Yeah, I want to get some experience." The idea of working – just to be 'in a movie' – was very important to me ten years ago. And I needed the money.

'The fact that people capitalize on something like that seems to be a function of modern society. That couldn't happen a hundred and fifty years ago,' he added somewhat pompously. 'Those people would have had to answer to me personally in terms of real justice and not something that's litigated. These two movies are classic examples of somebody with no experience being in pictures no matter what they were like.' But he added: 'That's all in the past now. I don't look back. Only forward.'

Chapter Seven

Moving On

IN 1991 Kevin Costner appeared for the first time on *Forbes* magazine's annual list of the Top 40 Highest-Paid Entertainers Of The Year. Coming straight in at number six with an estimated $50 million, he led the field of film stars which included such other Hollywood stalwarts as Arnold Schwarzenegger ($15 million), Sean Connery ($14 million) and Sylvester Stallone ($10 million). Although his pay cheques were now averaging $8 million a movie, most of the money he had earned was derived from the *Dances With Wolves* profits which had reached combined world box-office and video sales of

Kevin and Cindy Costner at the premiere of *JFK*. Cindy encouraged her husband to take on the controversial role of Jim Garrison and her influence continues to be crucial.

around $500 million. According to *Variety*, as co-producer, director and star Costner's 'eventual payout should approach the $50 million earned by Jack Nicholson on *Batman*'. Indeed so popular had the movie become, it had been released again in December as *Dances With Wolves: The Special Edition* by way of celebration. The extra 52 minutes of new material in this extended version brought the running time to almost four hours. The added scenes, which were shot for the eventual television screening of the film, gave a fuller explanation of some gaps in the story, such as the reasons why Dunbar found his outpost deserted and the torture and killing of a group of white settlers by the Sioux shortly before the big buffalo hunt. Costner insisted that this was 'due to public demand rather than a simple desire to cash in'.

Costner's popularity had reached unimaginable new heights due to the success of *Dances With Wolves* and *Robin Hood: Prince Of Thieves*. He was hailed as Hollywood's premier leading man, proclaimed the world's Number One Star. But with this new found fame he became a new kind of superstar – which Americans refer to as a 'supermarket celebrity' – and Costner found this hard to take. Like Elizabeth Taylor's multi-marriages and Michael Jackson's plastic surgery, his private life had now become as important as his film roles to certain factions of the press – so much so that Costner complained that he could no longer open up a magazine without his face staring up at him from its pages.

The tabloids weren't stupid – they had learned fast that Costner sold copies. However, Costner's 'Mr Clean' screen image made him an easy target for ridicule, and since the revelations of his alleged affairs during the filming of *Robin Hood*, the ever-eager gossip columnists had taken great delight in reporting even the slightest whispers about his off-screen activities. 'Let's face it, the public can only take this good-guy story about me for just so long,' Costner admitted. 'It's wearing thin. I feel over-exposed right now. People say I should shut it down. If I never did another day of press and publicity, it wouldn't bother me. I can see it coming to an end. I'm becoming more of a recluse.'

These comments of Costner's were borne out by the British journalist Garth Pearce, one of only a handful of reporters allowed on the closed set of *Robin Hood: Prince Of Thieves*. Pearce, author of the official book about the making of the movie, claimed that 'even getting to talk to Costner during filming was

hard work. There were constant grumblings that his ego has become so inflated he will only talk to the most important people on the set – and only then through his 23-year old blonde personal assistant.' Pearce added: 'I was treated to a 45-minute phone call with the same secretary over what Kevin did and didn't want printed. Things like his falling out with director Kevin Reynolds.'

According to film writer Maureen Dowd, who had interviewed Costner for *The New York Times* in June 1991, the change in the star had become very self-evident. In her opinion his 'roguish gleam' had all but disappeared in favour of 'a tiresome thirtysomething earnestness and smugness'. Summing up their conversation with the following statement, she suggested that Kevin should stop taking himself so seriously: 'It has been said that Mr Costner is worried about his thinning hair. His hair looks OK. It's his thinning skin he should be worried about.' *The Hollywood Reporter*'s Martin Grove commented that Costner 'has become the *bête noir* for the media.' While his fellow critic, *The Washington Post*'s Tom Shales, dubbed him 'the Prince of Sanctimony'.

Pop star Madonna also had a go at Costner in her controversial documentary *Truth Or Dare* (*In Bed With Madonna* in Britain). The uncomfortable looking actor is seen visiting backstage after a concert and telling Madonna her show was 'neat'. After he leaves her dressing room Madonna sticks her fingers down her throat and makes a gagging sound. Costner was furious that he had been made a fool of and claimed that the singer had set him up. 'I don't know why I was in the film,' he fumed. 'They gave us [Costner and wife Cindy] tickets. She invited us. I don't know why she should do that.' Either way, the press had a field day and the story was picked up on by most publications with some even describing it as the 'best bit to watch out for' in the movie. Later *Variety* reported that Madonna had gone after the co-starring role in *The Bodyguard*, the film Costner began filming in November 1991. Rumour had it that Costner had insisted Madonna did not get the part.

It is not surprising, then, that Costner's attitude to the press had become noticeably more sour. His every move was under constant scrutiny. He could not do anything without it being dragged through the pages of the newspapers. For instance, it was widely publicised that Costner had played golf with President Bush and tennis star André Agassi at Camp David in July of 1991 and had then gone back to the White House for lunch. But one of Costner's 'closest [though unnamed] associates' claimed that George Bush had been calling Costner every day since to arrange another game, without success. Another ludicrous claim was that Costner had paid $350 for a vast quantity of chocolate to be placed in the refrigerator of his Washington, D.C. hotel room.

Yet another report claimed that Costner had 'informed' Whitney Houston of his intention to sing with her on five of the songs she was to record for the soundtrack of the *The Bodyguard*. With it came the revelation that Costner had recorded an album three years earlier which had been released only in Japan. It turned out that since the mid-eighties, Costner had been singer and lead guitarist of a four-piece country rock group called Roving Boy. Along with band members Blair Forward, Steve Appel and

John Coinmen, their 1988 album *The Simple Truth* had reached number 67 in the Japanese domestic music charts; the title track also featured as the 'theme song' on a Japanese television mini-series, *Dun-Huang*, and was later used on the soundtrack of a Suntory malt beer commercial.

'I don't tell people all the things I do,' Costner said. 'Music is very private to me. I have to be very careful how it's handled.' Making the album had been rather like a hobby for him. He only allowed it to be released in Japan by the Tokuma Group because 'that is what I felt most comfortable with. My singing and recording career has not been a long-time dream, rather a long-time pursuit.'

Like many celebrities who make lucrative but lurid Japanese commercials that they wouldn't allow to be seen at home – such as Paul Newman's coffee advertisement and Charlie Sheen plugging training shoes – Costner was content to air his singing abilities so long as it was confined to overseas markets. But a copy of *The Simple Truth* album had managed to find its way to America – and on to the sound system of *Los Angeles Times* music critic Robert Hillburn. 'Let's put it this way,' Hillburn said, 'if recent albums by Don Johnson and Bruce Willis represented the "good" and "bad" in celebrity pop performances, it's not stretching things too far to say that Costner's album represents the "ugly".' Hillburn continued: 'Willis at least had the good sense to do playful remakes of R&B classics, whereas Costner takes himself seriously with original material. Anyway, even if Costner had given a performance on the level of Bruce Willis, it wouldn't be saying much.'

'Kevin sings for his supper' is how the *Daily Express* headlined Costner's intention to make his stage debut in a musical. The British newspaper reported that the actor was working with composer-producer Richard Baskin, heir to the Baskin-Robbins ice cream empire, on 'a musical with a South American theme'. 'It's premature to make any announcements. We haven't even hired a writer,' said Baskin. Baskin refused to be drawn on Costner's singing abilities: 'That's something you'll have to wait to find out,' he said.

Costner paid a backstage visit to another pop star that year when Paul McCartney visited Los Angeles. Costner was one of the few stars there whom McCartney had really enjoyed meeting. McCartney had described Costner as 'very down-to-earth' and 'a really nice guy' and added that he admired him for the determination he had shown in getting *Dances With Wolves* made.

In a despatch from Dallas, where Costner had been on location filming *JFK*, the British tabloid the *Sunday Mirror* alleged that Costner and the film's director Oliver Stone had enjoyed two nights together watching go-go dancers perform a topless strip act at the city's high-class Cabaret Royale Club. The reporter claimed that the pair had offered some of the girls dancing roles in the movie. The club owner, Salah Izzedin, said: 'Kevin was treated like a king and enjoyed every minute. We laid on our most expensive champagne – and the girls were dancing right up close to him.'

Another British tabloid, the *Daily Star*, claimed that Costner had 'gone back to nature...dancing naked with male pals'. The article revealed that Costner and ten of his friends had spent a week in the wilds of Wyoming living off the land like Indians and taking part in a male bonding ritual which involved dancing naked to the beat of drums around their camp fire. Costner and his friends were inspired by the bestselling book *Iron John* by Robert Bly, which suggested that men were losing their essential masculinity and needed to get away from women to experience a rugged lifestyle. According to followers of Robert Bly's philosophy there was no homosexual element in these bonding rituals. It is said to release men from female-dominated home life and make them feel like warriors again.

While Costner was filming *JFK* on location in Dallas, the *Dallas Morning News* ran a 'Kevin Watch' column. Thrilled that a movie star was filming in their city, the newspaper had asked that anyone who had seen Kevin out and about in Dallas should write in with their experience. 'I kept thinking to myself, "He looks so familiar",' wrote one woman as she described in minute detail serving the star at her store in the city's West End shopping mall. Then, when she had realised who it was... 'And I went, "Oh, my god, really!" From then on, I was so nervous... He charged $450 of merchandise on his gold American Express card. And I was like, "Oh, I'm touching his card."' Another woman, a bank employee, told how her office overlooked the *JFK* lot where Kevin's trailer had been parked. 'We all have our binoculars,' she reported. 'I'd say from all the women looking out the windows the whole building is leaning over to one side.'

Whether the stories were true or not was hardly the point as far as Costner was concerned. The fact that the reports had

Kevin Costner (centre) at the
premiere of *JFK*, with (left to right)
Jack Lemmon, director Oliver
Stone, and Sissy Spacek who
played Jim Garrison's wife in the
movie.

found their way into print in the first place
was what he had found the most disturbing.
'I get a sickening feeling when someone
comes up to me and says, "I read something
about you." My pits start to sweat when
somebody says [that]. Why do I have to go
through that?' Costner asked coldly. 'I like
what I do, but it's too bad I get all the money
I get for it and it's too bad everybody has to
write about it. It's too bad people have to pan
it or give it endorsements. It's too bad we
depend on that.'

The press coverage wasn't all negative,
however. Stories of Costner's kindness and
generosity were also plentiful. When the
husband of the hairdresser on *Dances With
Wolves* died, Costner paid for the funeral

arrangements and the transportation of the
body from Dakota to Atlanta. He also
donated $120,000 to create a permanent
Sioux Indian exhibit at the South Dakota
Cultural Heritage Centre in Pierre. Costner,
who had been adopted by the Sioux nation
because of his honest portrayal of their tribe
on screen, had decided to donate the money
because of the reception he and his wife had
received while making the movie.

During *Robin Hood*, one of the crew
members had been forced to collect money
to pay the medical bills for his seriously ill
child. 'Kevin told him whatever money he
raised he would double it,' said Caroline Sax,
the script supervisor, in *Vanity Fair* magazine.
'And he was not doing that to impress
anyone.'

In New Orleans, where he had been
working on other scenes for *JFK*, Costner
was said to have 'rescued' a starving mother
he had seen stealing a pint of milk to feed her
hungry baby. He reputedly handed her all the
money he was carrying, around $200, then

went back into the supermarket to pay for the milk. Again in New Orleans, it was reported that the sympathetic star had made 'the last wish of a dying teenager come true'. In 'true Robin Hood spirit', the Spanish-owned magazine *Hello!* revealed how Kevin had learned that a 14-year-old local boy, Sean Dunlap, had only a week to live and wouldn't be able to fulfil his one last wish of seeing *Robin Hood: Prince Of Thieves*, which had yet to open in the city. Apparently 'caring family man Kevin' had set up a special screening of the film and had sat next to Sean throughout.

There has to be the sneaking suspicion that the release of stories like these were possibly orchestrated to counteract the bad press Costner had suffered after revelations about his involvement in extra-marital sex. As he had so ruefully found out, his self-imposed silence after these reports had served only to stir up further speculation about his private life. Like it or not, Costner had been forced to accept that this invasion of privacy by the press came part and parcel with being a celebrity.

Since his success with *Dances With Wolves* Costner's career had been steeped in controversy. His decision to star in *JFK*, the film that followed *Robin Hood*, added to his notoriety. Based on the assassination of American President John F. Kennedy, Oliver Stone's film had been widely criticised for bending the truth to support the theory of Jim Garrison, the former New Orleans district attorney who had tried to prove that there had been a conspiracy to kill Kennedy.

Oliver Stone, whose films include *Wall Street*, *Platoon*, *Born On The Fourth Of July* and *The Doors*, had called Costner while he was in London filming *Robin Hood* and asked him to play Garrison. At first Costner had been hesitant, and had insisted that Stone send him a copy of the script first before they met to discuss the project. 'Oliver came on a plane to England with his first *JFK* script. He was like a mortar coming for me,' Costner recalled. 'We talked – but I was thinking, I don't look like this Garrison guy, why does he want me to play him?' Having learned to trust his wife Cindy's judgement, Costner had then passed the script on to her with his deep misgivings. 'Cindy and I had reached the point where we'd decided to take three or four months off. We'd put a lot of energy into *Dances With Wolves*, and then there was *Robin Hood* – a very rough shoot in England. I was tired and I didn't feel I had the right even to propose it to Cindy. I told her that I just didn't feel so strongly about this movie that I'd upset our big plans to go away together camping in the mountains with our kids.' But Kevin was surprised when Cindy told him that he should do it. 'She's never been so outspoken about something in my career, she was very forceful about it,' he said. 'I knew that she felt it was that important. She knew I was on the fence. She felt it was about the country, and I ultimately came to feel the same.'

John F. Kennedy was assassinated on 22 November 1963 as his open limousine sped along Dealey Plaza in Dallas, Texas. The findings of the Warren Commission, which had been set up to investigate the murder, concluded in 1965 that there had been no conspiracy and that the crime had been committed by a crazed gunman named Lee Harvey Oswald, a Marxist who was shot to death himself two days later by a vengeful nightclub owner Jack Ruby. Garrison disagreed with the Commission's verdict and brought to trial International Trade Mart Director Clay Shaw, a homosexual whom he had accused of taking part in the alleged conspiracy. Garrison's prosecution was hampered by the mysterious deaths of key witnesses, the disappearance of documents, hostility by the media and from the federal government. The case against Clay was thrown out of court after a jury acquitted him in less than one hour and Garrison was tagged as a 'flake' and an 'irresponsible publicity seeker' for tainting the reputation of the respected New Orleans businessman.

In a press conference shortly before the film's U.S. release in December 1991, Costner defended Garrison and the humiliation he had suffered at the hands of the American press. Bitter about the bad press he had received himself, Costner again drew parallels with his own life: 'I know the attacks that all of us receive,' he said. 'If I look at my life personally, I know that if I'm attacked my friends very rarely speak up for me in terms of the press. This is what my friends do: "Kevin, they're fulla shit. Don't worry about it." I tell you, men are of clay. They are all things. It's tough to know, but it's important to know.'

Costner added: 'I would not doubt that Jim Garrison is ambitious, but I do know that he's a patriot. He did trash this guy's life, but maybe that was an acceptable loss for bringing something to the light of day. Jim Garrison has to live with that – not me.'

Oliver Stone has acknowledged that much of his film was based on Garrison's story; he had read Garrison's 1988 book, *On The Trail Of The Assassins*, while working on *Born On The Fourth Of July* in the Far East. 'I was very

shaken by it,' he recalled. 'I was deeply, deeply moved and appalled, and I optioned the book myself. I wanted to get this story out.' Stone also credits another book, Jim Marrs' *Crossfire: The Plot That Killed Kennedy* and various public sources of information. 'We're looking at the old evidence and will present alternative scenarios not only based on Jim's account, but from various sources,' he insisted.

In the three decades that have elapsed since Kennedy's death there are still many unanswered questions, doubts and suspicions held by the American public. A Gallup poll commissioned in 1991 by Warner Brothers, the distributor of *JFK,* revealed that 73 per cent of the nation disbelieved the Warren Commission's theory that Oswald had acted alone.

Costner had been in the Third Grade when Kennedy had died. 'I never was an ambulance-chaser type of personality,' he claimed. 'The thing that had a bigger impact was seeing Jack Ruby step out of the crowd and into History. My mom came to the school and told the principal.' While filming *Bull Durham* in 1988 Costner had said that he did not believe in the conspiracy theory. 'Maybe I believe in Lee Harvey Oswald because I can't believe we're so fucking corrupt – maybe I have to believe that,' he had insisted. After having heard Stone's evidence, he had changed his mind quite considerably: 'You could examine it point by point and discredit and dismantle everything in *JFK,* but the movie as a whole has an emotional truth.'

Costner had gone to the Texas School Book Depository in Dallas where Oswald had supposedly fired his fatal shots from the sixth floor window. But as an experienced marksman, looking down the barrel of a similar, bolt-action rifle had caused him to question the truth. He said: 'I discovered it was not an easy shot – it was plain impossible. And I remember thinking: "This could never have happened the way they said." Being there, at that window, made me feel better about doing the movie. What we really believe now is that it is very possible more than one person was involved – by definition that is a conspiracy. I believe our story. I believe there was a conspiracy to cover up the murder.' But, Costner added: 'I don't agree with everything Oliver Stone says. But I think what he has achieved with *JFK* is breathtaking. It is almost guerilla film-making. I support him fully on this film. Oliver is more of a patriot than people expect.'

Oliver Stone was intent on showing that corruption involving the FBI, CIA and the government had resulted in Kennedy's murder and a subsequent cover-up. He insisted that 'there were sinister forces at work that killed him because he was seeking to change things'. And it was Costner, Stone felt, who would best give justice to the Garrison role. 'Kevin is a highly underrated actor in the sense that it's very subtle what he's doing,' he explained. 'Kevin's presence, like Gary Cooper's, is a very relaxed one. He's comfortable with himself. He serves my function perfectly, because he anchors the movie in integrity and honesty and he's also extremely watchable. He took some chances making this movie, he's going to make enemies, but I'm proud of him.'

From the moment the filming of *JFK* began in April 1991, boot-legged copies of its first-draft script had been widely available. Early criticism of Stone's accuracy and motives were aired in a clutch of condescending articles. In his lengthy feature entitled 'Dallas In Wonderland', *The Washington Post*'s George Lardner Jr slated the script for its many 'errors and absurdities'. While *The Chicago Tribune*'s Jon Margolis called it an 'insult to intelligence and decency'. Tony Burton, in New York for the British *Daily Mail*, declared that 'even while the film was still being edited by Stone, his vision was contested as a fairy story. Was it fair to distort historical events on film? Wasn't he exploiting a national tragedy?' Burton's colleague on the *Daily Mail*, gossip columnist Baz Bamigboye, revealed that the Princess of Wales had been 'banned' from attending the London premiere of the film, prior to the film's release in Britain in January 1992. 'Palace advisers,' he claimed, 'had told the Princess that the film is not suitable to be endorsed by a member of the Royal Family.' Bamigboye added: 'The Palace decision is disappointing for Diana, who was keen to meet the film's star, Hollywood golden boy Kevin Costner.' Pierre Salinger, a former press secretary for both Kennedy and his predecessor Lyndon Johnson, and now a world renowned writer, decried the movie in the London *Evening Standard* as a 'travesty and something an honest movie director should never have put together ... So why is Oliver Stone producing a film which is a major lie?' These comments were echoed by former American President Gerald Ford, who had served on the Warren Commission. He described *JFK* as 'a desecration of the memory of President Kennedy and a fraudulent misrepresentation of the truth'.

Kevin Costner as Jim Garrison taking a break off-set during the shooting of *JFK*, with Donald Sutherland, who played the CIA officer known in the movie simply as 'X'.

If the facts were questionable, the authenticity of the scenes in the $35 million movie were beyond reproach. Dallas County commissioners had allowed Stone to film in the former Texas School Book Depository; the site of the assassin's perch, in what is now the County Administration Building, was converted into a museum in 1989 by the Dallas County Historical Foundation, displaying memorabilia on the life, presidency and assassination of Kennedy. This attention to detail became even more apparent when Stone had Dealey Plaza turned into a replica of what it was on the day Kennedy was killed. Trees were pruned to their height of 28 years before, signs erected and vintage cars parked on the street. And Costner, with the aid of clever make-up, was transformed into a bespectacled middle-aged man with greying temples to look like Garrison.

Even before it had been released *JFK* had become one of the most talked about films in years. In addition to Costner, the film boasted an impressive supporting cast including Jack Lemmon, Walter Matthau, Gary Oldman, Tommy Lee Jones, Donald Sutherland, Sissy Spacek, John Candy, Joe Pesci, Kevin Bacon and, in a bitter twist of irony, the real Jim Garrison playing Earl Warren, the chairman presiding over the Warren Commission. With a running time of three hours and ten minutes, this powerful and absorbing film never flags for a moment as Stone painstakingly tried to piece together what he called 'the jigsaw puzzle'; his dense, flashback-laden autopsy of the events leading up to and the aftermath of the slaying show just how awesome a task the director had chosen to undertake.

'The movie is actually four movies,' he explained. 'It's about Garrison in New Orleans; it's a recreation of the motorcade in Dealey Plaza; it's Lee Harvey Oswald and his story; and it's the deeper background to the whole thing back in Washingon D.C., where the power really is. We show the facts as they happen that day. We show the Oswald arrest, the Ruby killing, and we lay it all out. The speculations are clear to the audience as simply speculations. The movie is a hypothesis, based on fact.'

Newsreel footage was interspersed with recreated scenes and fiction, but Stone had been worried that the sheer magnitude and scope of information he had bombarded the audience with would in the end confuse them. 'The main style was to get to the point and not waste time – flash, flash, cut, cut –

Costner, on location in 1991 for Oliver Stone's *JFK*, tries out a police motorcycle to the amusement of the officers on duty. While some have criticised Costner's aloofness, he has also been capable of great acts of personal generosity.

and always come back to things,' Stone continued. 'Good teachers know that repetition is a good way to teach and there is so much information in the movie that no matter how intelligent you are, you're going to lose a piece of it first time through.'

Despite this sporadic, documentary-style approach, Stone had managed to spin an intricate web of intrigue and suspense that sucked in audiences and left them guessing. At the final frame, the expectant epilogue concluded that the now dead Clay had in fact been working for the CIA after all as Garrison had claimed, and that the findings of a later commission, which had re-examined the facts in the late seventies, had admitted that there was a 'probable conspiracy'. With the all important FBI and CIA documents relating to the events remaining under lock and key until the year 2029, ultimately one is still left wondering who, and indeed why it all happened.

As Garrison Costner gave one of his honest 'all-American' performances, his grand finale in the shape of a long, sweeping courtroom speech reminiscent of James Stewart at his idealistic best in Capra's *Mr Smith Goes To Washington*. Almost breaking down with emotion, Costner's voice wavers and croaks as his presence in the film comes belatedly to the fore to dominate the final scenes. 'That speech was how I could buy into the movie at some level,' Costner said. 'It was never intended to be emotional. There was no direction like "He breaks down here." Those tears came from the whole weight of the movie, of being oppressed, of being made a fool of. I absorbed myself into being the guy. I was as surprised as anybody, because the words read almost corny.'

Costner continued: 'I know how exhausted that man must've been. Remember when Richard Dreyfuss saw the space ship [in *Close Encounters Of The Third Kind*]? He's a pretty normal guy. His life was fucked up forever because he saw something he could never say he didn't see. And that's the way I played it. I hope I never see a UFO. You're gonna end up on the top of the heap if you take on the US Government, so there's no pot of gold at the end of the rainbow. But sometimes people in their lives say I don't care – I've just gotta go forward.'

Tommy Lee Jones, who played the plaintiff Clay Shaw, justified the need to make the movie. '*Of course* it's necessary to make the film. *Of course* it matters,' he insisted at the press conference for *JFK*, which was also attended by most of the film's main stars including Costner. 'Films can certainly affect people's social and political thinking. You know that as well as I do. Films are feared by those who would control our social and political thinking for their own reasons. You know *that*.'

Sissy Spacek, superb in the part of Garrison's wife Liz, said: 'I know when I read the script I was very shaken and frightened to think there was a possibility that something sinister happened. It really shook me up, and

after doing my own research I think it's highly probable.' She added: 'I'm not sure how this movie is going to affect public perception or memory.'

Support for Oliver Stone, winner of the 1992 Golden Globe Award for Best Director for *JFK* (which won two 1992 Academy Awards for Best Cinematography and Best Film Editing), was reflected in an over-whelming vote of confidence from critics. 'Stunning. Powerful. Remarkable. It holds the audience rapt in its grip,' said David Ansen in *Newsweek*. 'A masterpiece. Hypnotic, it grips and disturbs,' declared Roger Ebert in the *Chicago Sun-Times*. 'Electrifying. A knockout. Breathless. Enthralling. Sensa-tional. Terrific,' wrote Richard Corliss in *Time*. 'A smash hit. *JFK* will endure as a must-see for years,' said Mike Clark in *USA Today*. 'Masterful filmmaking, a staggering achievement. It keeps you on the edge of your seat. Kevin Costner is excellent,' said Joel Siegel on 'Good Morning America', ABC-TV. 'Kevin Costner, ideal for the part, radiates decency and trustability as Garrison,' wrote Shaun Usher in the *Daily Mail*, who added: 'Yes, *JFK* is propaganda packaged as high-voltage tension, intrigue and human drama. Angry and accusatory enough to escape charge of exploiting tragedy, is also the year's first unmissable film.'

Costner expressed concern about one aspect of the renewed controversy surrounding *JFK*. 'The only thing I really regret is that the Kennedys have to be drawn into the public eye,' he said.

Kevin Costner has long been known for his conservative political views. He joined the Republican party when he was 21 and had reportedly backed Republican Senator Phil

Gramm of Texas with $4,000 for his 1996 bid for the Presidential race. Costner has often declared himself to be 'a Bush supporter' and has claimed that the President has 'been a friend to me'. Knowing that George Bush was a former head of the CIA, he was also well aware of the speculation his association with *JFK* would bring. 'He has never asked me to do anything for him,' Costner said guardedly of President Bush. 'And he never questioned this movie.' Costner stated firmly: 'I would ask you to be specifically clear about this because it is obviously a very delicate matter for him. I don't tell him how to do his job and he doesn't presume to tell me how to do mine. I don't think he's the kind of person who is threatened by a movie like *JFK* – although it seems a lot of Americans are.'

The legacy of the Kennedy controversy continued to shadow Costner even as his next project after *JFK* went into production. The set of *The Bodyguard* was closed to all but trusted cast and crew members after its star had received several death threats. Due to a series of menacing telephone calls condemning him for taking the part of Garrison, it had been reported that Costner himself had been forced to hire his own bodyguards.

The Bodyguard is a slick romantic thriller about a star who falls in love with her minder, Frank Farmer, played by Costner in a crew cut. Farmer is a highly-paid personal bodyguard, one of the best in a very dangerous field. The former Secret Service agent has met every professional challenge while protecting high-profile clients from congressmen to business moguls. But that was before he was hired to shield the glamorous Rachel Marron (Whitney Houston), a performer whose popularity has made her a star but brought her the negative trappings of fame as well: the over-protective entourage and now, the unwanted attention of an obsessive fan who threatens not only her life, but the lives of those around her.

Farmer's expertise in personal security is tested by his latest client. In setting up a tight security routine for the singer, he finds that intimate contact with her brings him to the brink of breaking his own rule: never mix business with pleasure.

Elaborate preparations were put into motion by production designer Jeffrey Beecroft (who also worked on *Dances With Wolves*) to recreate not only the opulence of Rachel Marron's lifestyle but the reality of her celebrity. This included mounting an entire Academy Awards ceremony complete with limos, paparazzi and fans waiting outside the doors while a thousand extras in evening wear gathered inside the Pantages Theater in Hollywood for the mock 'Oscars'.

Kevin Costner's character is also based in reality, as several top professional bodyguards were consulted about Frank Farmer's world. Costner took instruction in such diverse areas as knife-throwing, surveillance electronics and martial arts to bring authenticity to Farmer's actions on screen.

Whitney Houston performed several songs in the film and stars in a music video shot by director Mick Jackson, which is integrated into the film. There are several new songs as well as several of Whitney Houston's past hits on the soundtrack. She had been searching for some time for a suitable part in which to break into movies, and *The Bodyguard* seemed ideal.

A Tig Production, Costner co-produced

Director Oliver Stone (left) lightens the tense on-set atmosphere with Costner, by pretending to straighten his tie between takes on *JFK*.

the film with his long-time collaborator Lawrence Kasdan (who also wrote the screenplay) and Jim Wilson. 'Kevin wanted to work with Whitney and it's a tremendous role for her,' said Wilson. Costner had been impressed by Whitney Houston's pop videos and the way she handled herself in television interviews, saying that she 'commanded attention with her poise and grace'. The singer said that Costner had been determined she get the part, despite her inexperience. 'Kevin said to me, "I know you can do it; I know you can act. I want you".' Houston added: 'There's room for a coach, but no

acting lessons. I've always been an actress – when you perform on stage you act.'

When Costner was seen kissing his co-star behind a trailer on the set of *The Bodyguard*, the 'coach' claimed that 'we were rehearsing a love scene! She needed help. She's never made a movie before. She was hired for the role on the strength of her name. No screen test. I thought I'd help where I can. Kissing scenes are very hard to do convincingly, even for me.'

But Whitney Houston backed out of doing nude scenes with Kevin Costner. It had been reported that she had second thoughts after a heart-to-heart with her mother. Instead she wore a special body stocking for the love scenes which were filmed in silhouette to make it look as if she was naked. 'I just couldn't do it. My mother would have killed me,' she told the British *Daily Mirror*, to which the deeply religious Cissy Houston, a noted Gospel singer, retorted: 'I don't care how much Whitney wants to be in movies. She shouldn't even *pretend* to be naked. It just isn't right.'

Although *The Bodyguard* marked the third project that Costner had made within a year for Warner Brothers, it was not until he began filming the movie that the signing of an exclusive new contract with Warners was confirmed. The new agreement gave Costner the right to direct, develop, produce and star in films for the studio. Through Tig Productions Costner had already been contracted to Orion Pictures, so the announcement also brought a certain amount of controversy with it.

Costner had formed Tig Productions with his close friend Jim Wilson in the summer of 1989. By 1990 they had signed a lucrative deal with Orion Pictures. 'I have made Orion my creative home [because] of the enormously satisfying experience I had making *No Way Out* and *Bull Durham*,' Costner declared at the time. The terms of their arrangement stipulated that Costner would produce and/or star in films for the studio through Tig Productions. *Dances With Wolves* was their first venture, produced and financed independently under contract, but distributed by Orion. After the success of *Dances With Wolves*, Tig was inundated with scripts and decided to develop two further projects, *Mick* and *American Hero*. *Mick* was another controversial subject which Costner had chosen to become involved with. He had planned to direct himself in the title role of the period film which was to be based on the life of Michael Collins, a founding father of republican Ireland. The title of *American Hero*

had all the hallmarks of a typical Costner-starring vehicle, but no actual details of its development had been made known. Then the situation changed dramatically.

As his contract with Orion had allowed him the freedom to make films for other studios, Costner had then become involved with Warner Brothers. But as *Variety* confirmed in May of 1991, he had also relocated his production facilities to the Warner Brothers lot at Burbank. Rumours were rife that Costner and Wilson were deserting the ailing Orion which had been struck with serious financial problems. *Variety* reported in July that Costner had not received his fair share of the profits from *Dances With Wolves*. They claimed he had received only $7.5 million and not the estimated $50 million he was entitled to. A spokesman for Costner denied the report, but *Variety* countered with the claim that Costner is 'worried about being stalled and that his agent, Creative Artists Agency's head Mike Ovitz, has been putting the pressure on Orion to collect what's due'.

Although Orion had scored major box-office successes with *Dances With Wolves* and *The Silence Of the Lambs*, they had been forced to sell *The Addams Family* to Paramount Pictures for a mere $24 million in a last-ditch effort to fight off the receivers. Ironically *The Addams Family* would gross $67 million within three weeks for Paramount, but by that time it had been much too late for Orion. With reported debts in excess of $700 million, at the beginning of 1992 the company filed for Chapter 11 protection from its creditors. In addition, Orion had retained the rights to *Mick* and *American Hero*. As Jim Wilson had stated after Costner's departure that 'any other projects that had been developed within Orion will be distributed by the company', both projects looked doomed to be forgotten.

Nevertheless, Costner was reportedly 'thrilled' with the Warner Brothers alliance, and with Mike Ovitz now guiding his career, he had continued to go from strength to strength. 'Mike Ovitz is the single most powerful agent in the business, and Kevin felt he needed things that Ovitz's power could provide,' said J.J. Harris, Costner's agent until 1989. Mike Ovitz, who was also the agent for Sean Connery and Glenn Close among many others, came in at No. 1 in the Premiere ranking of the 100 most powerful people in Hollywood for 1991, and Costner was ranked at No. 13.

Always one step ahead, Costner was seldom without a number of films in discussion or development at any one time. While filming *JFK*, he had been negotiating for the title role in *Nostradamus*, a Franco-American adaptation of *La Vie Fabuleuse De Nostradamus*, to be directed by Kenneth Branagh. Costner was planning to film *Benya The King,* the Isaac Babel book set during the Russian revolution which he would direct and star in. And of course, there was also *Camelot*, the film Costner had been talking about remaking for years. 'The role I'd really love to play is King Arthur. No kiddin',' he said, his face alive with boyish enthusiasm. 'I started singing in choir at school, in musicals. Richard Harris I loved; he sings with great commitment, and I don't imagine that Arthur was that great a singer. I just imagine him as being a really good man who is faced with incredible dilemmas.'

One could well imagine Kevin Costner as Arthur, even if it did mean he had to sing. But gone are the hungry years when he had been happy to accept anything that came his way. Costner may have completed three films back-to-back in the space of a year, but he was also a star who was conscious of burning himself out. With the power to produce and direct films, as well as starring in them, he could afford to be selective about which projects to do next, something reflected in his future choice of film roles. But in the end, when all is said and done, it is really only Kevin Costner who can say what is right for him:

'I don't know what the public expects of me, but I know what I expect from myself and that's really all it's about. I don't have a career by design, where I try to anticipate trends or guess what audiences are going to love. I do films because I love them when I read the script.

'Sure, I'm successful now, but in the long haul, the way I see it is that your run in Hollywood can be like a sprint – whereas your whole life is a marathon. I never anticipated being the Number One guy; I don't have that kind of attitude. The way it is now is not the way it will always be.

'I also believe you have to leave a window open for opportunity, for something to happen in your life. Who knows what may turn up? Perhaps it won't even be in movies. If I tied my life up in advance for the next two years, I would miss out if something much more important came along – and that might not even be a movie, you know? I could easily live in Alaska on a river and mine gold. And trap and hunt. Very easily. Life is a journey. I do reserve the right to change my life if I so desire.'

Filmography

[Dates refer to year of release]

Stacy's Knights (1981)
Director: Jim Wilson
Produced by JoAnn Locktov and
   Freddy Sweet
Screenplay by Michael Blake
Music by Norton Buffalo
Director of Photography: Raoul
   Lomas
Crown
Cast: Andra Millian (*Stacy Lancaster*),
   Kevin Costner (*Will Bonner*), Eve
   Lilith (*Jean Dennison*), Mike
   Reynolds (*Shecky Poole*), Ed Semenza
   (*The Kid*), Garth Howard (*Mr C*)

Frances (1982)
Director: Graeme Clifford
Produced by Jonathan Sanger
Screenplay by Eric Bergren,
   Christopher DeVore and Nicholas
   Kazan
Music by John Barry
Director of Photography: Laszlo
   Kovacs
EMI/Brooksfilm-UNIV
Cast: Jessica Lange (*Frances Farmer*),
   Sam Shepard (*Harry York*), Kim
   Stanley (*Lillian Farmer*), Bart Burns
   (*Ernest Farmer*), James Brodhead
   (*Sergeant*), Kevin Costner (*Luther
   Adler;* cut from finished film)

One From The Heart (1982)
Director: Francis Ford Coppola
Produced by Dean Tavoularis
Screenplay by Armyan Bernstein and
   Francis Ford Coppola
Music by Tom Waits
Director of Photography: Vittorio
   Storaro
Zoetrope Studios
Cast: Frederic Forrest (*Hank*), Teri
   Garr (*Frannie*), Raul Julia (*Ray*),
   Nastassja Kinski (*circus acrobat*),
   Kevin Costner (part cut from final
   film)

Night Shift (1982)
Director: Ron Howard
Produced by Brian Grazer
Executive Producer: Don Kranze

Screenplay by Lowell Ganz and
   Babaloo Mandel
Music by Burt Bacharach
Director of Photography: James
   Crabe
Columbia-EMI-Warner
Cast: Henry Winkler (*Chuck Lumley
   III*), Michael Keaton (*Bill 'Billy
   Blaze' Blazejowski*), Shelley Long
   (*Belinda Keaton*), Gina Hecht
   (*Charlotte Koogle*), Pat Corely (*Edward
   Koogle*), Kevin Costner (*1st Frat Boy*)

The Big Chill (1983)
Director: Lawrence Kasdan
Produced by Michael Shamberg
Executive Producers: Marcia Nasatir
   and Lawrence Kasdan
Screenplay by Lawrence Kasdan and
   Barbara Benedek
Music Consultant: Meg Kasdan, plus
   extracts by various artists
Director of Photography: John Bailey
Columbia-EMI-Warner
Cast: Tom Berenger (*Sam*), Glenn
   Close (*Sarah*), Jeff Goldblum
   (*Michael*), William Hurt (*Nick*),
   Kevin Kline (*Harold*), Mary Kay
   Place (*Meg*), Meg Tilly (*Chloe*),
   JoBeth Williams (*Karen*), Kevin
   Costner (part cut from final film)

Testament (1983)
Director: Lynne Littman
Produced by Jonathan Bernstein and
   Lynne Littman
Screenplay by John Sacret Young
Based on the story *The Last Testament*
   by Carol Amen
Music by James Horner
Director of Photography: Steven
   Poster
Universal
Cast: Jane Alexander (*Carol Wetherly*),
   William Devane (*Tom Wetherly*),
   Ross Harris (*Brad Wetherly*), Roxana
   Zal (*Mary Liz Wetherly*), Lukas Hass
   (*Scottie Wetherly*), Philip Anglim
   (*Hollis*), Leon Ames (*Henry Abhart*),
   Rebecca De Mornay (*Cathy Pitkin*),

Kevin Costner (*Phil Pitkin*), Mico
   Olmos (*Larry*)

Table For Five (1983)
Director: Robert Lieberman
Produced by Robert Schaffel
Screenplay by David Seltzer
Music by Miles Goodman and John
   Morris
Director of Photography: Vilmos
   Zsigmond
CBS
Cast: Jon Voight (*J. P. Tannen*),
   Richard Crenna (*Mitchell*), Marie
   Christine Barrault (*Marie*), Millie
   Perkins (*Kathleen*), Roxana Zal
   (*Tilde*), Robby Kiger (*Truman-Paul*),
   Cynthia Kania, Kevin Costner
   (*Newly-weds*)

Shadows Run Black (1984)
Director: Howard Heard
Produced by Eric Louzil
Associate Producer: Laurel A.
   Koerning
Screenplay by Craig Kusaba and Duke
   Howard
Music by Steve Mann
Mesa Films
Cast: William J. Kulzer (*Rydell King*),
   Kevin Costner (*Jimmy Scott*),
   Elizabeth Trosper (*Judy Cole*), Shea
   Porter (*Morgan Cole*), George J.
   Engelson (*Priest*), Dianne Hinkler
   (*Helen Cole*)

Fandango (1984)
Director: Kevin Reynolds
Produced by Tim Zinnemann
Executive Producers: Frank Marshall
   and Kathleen Kennedy
Screenplay by Kevin Reynolds
Music by Alan Silvestri
Director of Photography: Thomas
   Del Ruth
Warner Brothers
Cast: Kevin Costner (*Gardner Barnes*),
   Judd Nelson (*Phil Hicks*), Sam
   Robards (*Kenneth Waggener*), Chuck
   Bush (*Dorman*), Brian Cesak (*Lester*),
   Marvin J. McIntyre (*Truman Sparks*)

American Flyers (1985)
Director: John Badham
Produced by Gareth Wigan and Paula
  Weinstein
Screenplay by Steve Tesich
Music by Lee Ritenour and Greg
  Mathieson
Warner Brothers
Cast: Kevin Costner (*Marcus
  Sommers*), David Grant (*David
  Sommers*), Rae Dawn Chong (*Sarah*),
  Alexandra Paul (*Becky*), Janice Rule
  (*Mrs Sommers*), John Amos (*Dr
  Conrad*), Robert Townsend (*Jerome*)

Silverado (1985)
Director: Lawrence Kasdan
Produced by Lawrence Kasdan
Executive Producers: Charles Okun
  and Michael Grillo
Screenplay by Lawrence Kasdan and
  Mark Kasdan
Music by Bruce Broughton
Director of Photography: John Bailey
Columbia-EMI-Warner
Cast: Kevin Kline (*Paden*), Scott
  Glenn (*Emmett*), Kevin Costner
  (*Jake*), Danny Glover (*Mal*), Brian
  Dennehy (*Cobb*), Linda Hunt
  (*Stella*), Jeff Goldblum (*Slick*),
  Rosanna Arquette (*Hannah*), John
  Cleese (*Sheriff Langston*)

Sizzle Beach, USA (1986)
Director: Richard Brander
Produced by Eric Louzil
Associate Producer: Laurel A.
  Koerning
Screenplay by Craig Kusaba
A Troma Release
Cast: Kevin Costner (*John Logan*),
  Terry Congie (*Janice*), Leslie Brander
  (*Sheryl*), Roselyn Royce (*Dit*)

No Way Out (1987)
Director: Roger Donaldson
Executive Producer: Mace Neufield
Produced by Laura Ziskin and Robert
  Garland
Screenplay by Robert Garland
Based on the novel *The Big Clock* by
  Kenneth Fearing
Music by Maurice Jarre
Directors of Photography: John Alcott
  and Alun Bollinger
Orion Pictures
Cast: Kevin Costner (*Tom Farrell*),

Gene Hackman (*David Brice*), Sean
  Young (*Susan Atwell*), Will Patton
  (*Scott Pritchard*), Howard Duff
  (*Senator Duvall*), George Dzundza
  (*Sam Hesselman*), Iman (*Nina Beka*)

The Untouchables (1987)
Director: Brian De Palma
Produced by Art Linson
Associate Producer: Ray Hartwick
Screenplay by David Mamet
Suggested by the television series and
  based on the works by Oscar Fraley
  with Eliot Ness and Paul Robsky
Music by Ennio Morricone
Director of Photography: Stephen H.
  Burum
Paramount
Cast: Kevin Costner (*Eliot Ness*), Sean
  Connery (*Jim Malone*), Charles
  Martin Smith (*Oscar Wallace*), Andy
  Garcia (*George Stone*), Robert De
  Niro (*Al Capone*)

Amazing Stories: The Mission
  (1987)
Director: Steven Spielberg
Executive Producer: Steven Spielberg
Screenplay by Menno Meyjes
Music by John Williams
Director of Photography: John
  McPherson
Universal
Cast: Kevin Costner (*Captain Spark*),
  Casey Siemaszko (*Jonathan*), Kiefer
  Sutherland (*Static*), Jeffrey Jay
  Cohen (*Jake*), John Philbin
  (*Bullseye*), Gary Mauro (*Sam*)

Bull Durham (1988)
Director: Ron Shelton
Produced by Thom Mount and Mark
  Burg
Screenplay by Ron Shelton
Music by Michael Convertino
Director of Photography: Bobby
  Byrne
Orion Pictures
Cast: Kevin Costner (*Crash Davis*),
  Susan Sarandon (*Annie Savoy*), Tim
  Robbins (*Ebby Calvin 'Nuke'
  LaLoosh*), Trey Wilson (*Joe 'Skip'
  Riggins*), Robert Wuhl (*Larry Hockett*)

Field of Dreams (1989)
Director: Phil Alden Robinson
Produced by Lawrence Gordon and
  Charles Gordon

Screenplay by Phil Alden Robinson
Based on the book *Shoeless Joe* by W.
  P. Kinsella
Music by James Horner
Director of Photography: John
  Lindley
Orion Pictures
Cast: Kevin Costner (*Ray Kinsella*),
  Amy Madigan (*Annie Kinsella*), Gaby
  Hoffman (*Karin Kinsella*), Ray Liotta
  (*Shoeless Joe Jackson*), Timothy
  Busfield (*Mark*), James Earl Jones
  (*Terence Mann*), Burt Lancaster (*Dr
  Archibald 'Moonlight' Graham*), Frank
  Whaley (*Archie Graham*)

Chasing Dreams (1989)
Director: Sean Roche
Produced by David G. Brown and
  Therese Conte
Screenplay by David G. Brown
Director of Photography: Connie
  Holt
Prism Entertainment
Cast: David G.Brown (*Gavin*), John
  Fife (*Parks*), Matthew Clark (*Ben*),
  Lisa Kingston (*Sue*), Jim Shane
  (*Father*), Claudia Carroll (*Mother*),
  Kevin Costner (*Brother*)

The Gunrunner (1989)
Director: Nardo Castillo
Produced by Richard Sadler and
  Robert J. Langevin
Screenplay by Arnie Gelbart
Music by Rex Taylor Smith
Director of Photography: Alain
  Dostie
New World-Video Voice
Cast: Kevin Costner (*Ted Beaubien*),
  Sara Botsford (*Maude*), Paul Soles
  (*Lochman*), Gerard Parkes (*Wilson*),
  Ron Lea (*George*), Mitch Martin
  (*Rosalyn*), Larry Lewis (*Robert*)

Revenge (1990)
Director: Tony Scott
Executive Producer: Kevin Costner
Producers: Hunt Lowry and Stanley
  Rubin
Screenplay by Jim Harrison and
  Jeffrey Fiskin
Based on the novella by Jim Harrison
Music by Jack Nitzsche
Director of Photography: Jeffrey
  Kimball
Columbia-New World

Cast: Kevin Costner (*Cochran*), Anthony Quinn (*Tibey*), Madeleine Stowe (*Miryea*), Tomas Milian (*Cesar*), Joaquin Martinez (*Mauro*), James Gammon (*Texan*), Jesse Corti (*Madero*), Sally Kirkland (*Rock star*), Miguel Ferrer (*Amador*)

Dances With Wolves (1990)
Director: Kevin Costner
Produced by Jim Wilson and Kevin Costner
Screenplay by Michael Blake,
Based on his novel *Dances With Wolves*
Music by John Barry
Director of Photography: Dean Semler
Orion Pictures
Cast: Kevin Costner (*Lt. John J. Dunbar*), Mary McDonnell (*Stands With A Fist*), Graham Greene (*Kicking Bird*), Rodney A. Grant (*Wind In His Hair*), Floyd Red Crow Westerman (*Ten Bears*), Tantoo Cardinal (*Black Shawl*), Jimmy Herman (*Stone Calf*), Nathan Lee (*Smiles A Lot*)

Robin Hood: Prince of Thieves (1991)
Director: Kevin Reynolds
Executive Producer: James G. Robinson
Executive Co-Producers: David Nicksay and Gary Barber
Produced by John Watson, Pen Densham and Richard B. Lewis
Screenplay by Pen Densham and John Watson
Based on a story by Pen Densham
Music by Michael Kamen
Director of Photography: Douglas Milsome
Warner Brothers
Cast: Kevin Costner (*Robin of Locksley*), Morgan Freeman (*Azeem*), Christian Slater (*Will Scarlet*), Alan Rickman (*Sheriff of Nottingham*), Mary Elizabeth Mastrantonio (*Marian*), Geraldine McEwan (*Mortianna*), Michael McShane (*Friar Tuck*), Lord Locksley (*Brian Blessed*), Michael Wincott (*Guy of Gisborne*), Nick Brimble (*John Little*), Daniel Newman (*Wulf*)

JFK (1991)
Director: Oliver Stone

Executive Producer: Arnon Milchan
Produced by A. Kitman Ho and Oliver Stone
Screenplay by Oliver Stone and Zachary Sklar
Based on the books *On The Trail Of The Assassins* by Jim Garrison and *Crossfire: The Plot That Killed Kennedy* by Jim Marrs
Music by John Williams
Director of Photography: Robert Richardson
Warner Brothers
Cast: Kevin Costner (*Jim Garrison*), Ed Asner (*Guy Bannister*), Jack Lemmon (*Jack Martin*), Gary Oldman (*Lee Harvey Oswald*), Sissy Spacek (*Liz Garrison*), Joe Pesci (*David Ferrie*), Walter Matthau (*Senator Long*), Tommy Lee Jones (*Clay Shaw*), John Candy (*Dean Andrews*), Kevin Bacon (*Willie O'Keefe*), Donald Sutherland (*X*)

The Bodyguard (1992)
Director: Mick Jackson
Produced by Lawrence Kasdan, Jim Wilson and Kevin Costner
Screenplay by Lawrence Kasdan
Music by David Foster
Director of Photography: Andrew Dunn
Warner Brothers
Cast: Kevin Costner (*Frank Farmer*), Whitney Houston (*Rachel Marron*), Bill Cobbs (*Bill Devaney*), Gary Kemp (*Sy Spector*), Michele Lamar Richards (*Nikki Marron*), Mike Starr (*Tony*)

Acknowledgements

I embarked upon this biography of Kevin Costner because, as a journalist working in show business, I was made aware of the demand for an accurate and up-to-date book about his career. I would therefore particularly like to thank Sandra Wake of Plexus Publishing for having the foresight and courage to give me the chance to write this book. I would like to express thanks to my editors, Nicky Adamson and Annette McFadyen; their ruthless blue pens have been a friend to me and I am grateful for it. Their insight and advice have been more helpful. I would also like to thank Terry Porter and Claire

Grainger for their work on this book, and special thanks are due to Simon Bell both for his creativity and his patience in designing the book – another day, another flat plan!

For their assistance along the way, I am most grateful to Sarah Thomas and David Linck of Warner Brothers and Andrew Dann of Guild Films. I would also like to thank Steve Gaul of Troma, Inc for his help and kind co-operation and for the use of stills from *Sizzle Beach, USA* and *Shadows Run Black*. I am indebted to Mike Wrenn for his advice. I would like to thank Maire Fahey and Frank Hopkinson for giving me my start as a writer. Thanks also to Sharon, Karen, Liz, Steve Mike.

A very special thanks to Jeff and Inge, Gregor and Dian, Gordon and Eleni, Jim, Alex, Margaret Potts, Billy Barr, Davie and Davina, Maria, Renee, Elizabeth, John and Ann Clark, Alison Brown, Patricia, Mota and Marianne Garcia for their interest and encouragement over the years.

Unfortunately Kevin Costner would not allow us to reproduce stills from *Dances With Wolves*, and we were also prevented from using stills from *Robin Hood: Prince of Thieves* and *JFK*. However we would like to thank the following for their co-operation in supplying photographs: Duncan Raban/All-Action Pictures; Bildarchiv, Munich; the British Film Institute; Frank Spooner Pictures Ltd; Matthew Nathans/Gamma Liaison; Bob Riha/Gamma; Stills, Paris; Retna Pictures; Mark Sennet/Onyx; Mark Hanauer/Onyx; Richard Corman/Tanner Associates/Onyx; Timothy White/Retna; David Strick/Retna; People in Pictures; Peter C. Borsari/People in Pictures; I. Wyman/Sygma; J. Markowitz/Sygma; Eddie Adams/Sygma; Trapper/Sygma; Guild Film Distribution. Film stills courtesy of: CBS, Columbia-EMI-Warner, Columbia-New World, Crown, EMI/Brooksfilm-UNIV, Mesa Films, New World-Video Voice, Orion Pictures, Paramount, Prism Entertainment, Troma, Universal, Warner Brothers, Zoetrope Studios.

Kelvin Caddies